## PRAISE FOR *MAKING SEN* *A PRACTICAL STATE-by-STATE APPROACH*

MW00849685

"Over the past 26 years, I have led our local teacher's union, and I have negotiated multiple contracts. These negotiations involved many aspects of school finance that I did not understand to the fullest extent. Countless times, I have questioned the accuracy of the district's treasurer; I have been unsure whether his or her answers were accurate, or if he or she was simply unable to articulate the answers. My curiosity and determination to find truth lead to my enrollment in a graduate program.

"While in the graduate program at Franciscan University of Steubenville, I had the opportunity to take several classes taught by Dr. Clinton Born, the author of *Making Sense of School Finance: A Practical State-by-State Approach.* Dr. Clinton Born's classes were very specific and informative. He made complex topics easy to understand by providing real-life applications using a 'no nonsense approach.' Dr. Born taught in a concise, intelligent, and transparent approach, and his book is no exception. In one easy-to-read source, Dr. Born covers all aspects of school finance revenue and accounting, while also exploring the funding programs in each state and the District of Columbia. There is no longer a need to consult multiple sources to find the answers to school finance questions in various states.

"Many authors talk the talk, but few have walked the walk. I believe because of his noted career in education and the quality of his research, Dr. Clinton Born is an expert in this field. I can honestly say this book will be the centerpiece of my professional library, and I urge all aspiring school administrators and practicing school employees to do the same."

—**Christopher Barto**, dean of students, Carrollton Elementary School, Carrollton Exempted Village School District, Carrollton, Ohio

"Dr. Clinton Born is a pioneer in the field of school finance and budgeting. His knowledge and expertise in many of these unchartered topics is vast and unparalleled. His book, *Making Sense of School Finance: A Practical State-by-State Approach*, unravels the complexity of school finance on a specific state basis for public, nonpublic, and public charter schools into clear, concise chapters that are easy to follow and understand. Aspiring superintendents, principals, and treasurers along with practicing school administrators will find this book an invaluable resource when acquiring and allocating school finances. This is the first book of its kind with specific state references, and Dr. Clinton Born explains every facet of what both new and seasoned administrators should know in school finance revenue and accounting procedures. This book truly makes sense out of cents!"

—**Dr. Wendy Hanasky**, co-owner, ACE Digital Academy

"*Making Sense of School Finance* is a true universal text and a must study for all aspiring and current school administrators. Dr. Clinton Born has written an incredible resource that provides an in-depth account of the important differences in the public school funding models used in each of the 50 states. Additionally, funding for each federal entitlement program as well as the information on nonpublic and public charter schools funding was valuable. The text is easy to read within a logical sequence, while challenging readers to make their own comparisons and develop their own conclusions. Data charts are provided in each chapter and authentic exhibits are available in the appendix, which serve as clear supplements to the reading."

—**John Poilek**, principal, Shadyside Local High School, Shadyside, Ohio

"Having recently completed Dr. Born's school finance class, I found that *Making Sense of School Finance* complemented the course's learning sessions and performance tasks. The unpublished text along with the course materials prepared me well for the weekly quizzes and other assignments. The text provides numerous pieces of data and charts to analyze information visually. It is a great, easy-to-read reference tool for novice and tenured school administrators."

—**Kayla DiMarzio**, chemistry/physics teacher and aspiring school administrator, Steubenville High School, Steubenville, Ohio

"*Making Sense of School Finance* is a text that every school administrator—both central office and building-level administrators—in America should read! Dr. Born provides an in-depth understanding of school finance that is applicable to all 50 states and the District of Columbia. This text is a one-stop-shop for anyone wanting to have a better grasp of how school finance works. The book provides real-world examples in a straightforward and uncomplicated fashion. This text is an excellent tool to understand the ins and outs of budgeting, revenue, and accounting at the local, state, and federal levels for school districts."

—**Stephanie Duffy-Zimmer**, PhD, director of technology and assessment, Brooke County Schools, Wellsburg, West Virginia

"As a new parochial school principal, *Making Sense of School Finance* offers a wonderful reference for nonpublic as well as public school finance. Most often, textbooks are geared toward public schools with limited mention of nonpublic or public charter schools. To see the inclusion of nonpublic and public charter school information in Dr. Born's text is refreshing because all education students in the university setting are not destined to work in a public school. As one of Dr. Born's students, I found that he makes a great effort to reference the nonpublic arena. Franciscan University of Steubenville, where Dr. Born teaches, is a Catholic university, so it was no surprise that he included this material in a book for aspiring administrators. I am sure that I will reference this book as I move through my administrative career."

—**Theresa A. Young**, principal, St. Mary
Central School, Martins Ferry, Ohio

"*Making Sense of School Finance* is a comprehensive resource for educational leaders. This book provides practical ideas on how to steward a school district's financial resources. Dr. Born begins each chapter with an overview of the understanding the reader should have by the end of the chapter. Further, Dr. Born facilitates the process of moving the reader beyond knowledge acquisition and into knowledge application by ending each chapter with projects and scenarios for discussion with colleagues.

"*Making Sense of School Finance* is chock-full of straightforward advice on a much-needed topic. I urge every CFO, superintendent, director of special education, and human resources director in the field of education to read this book and work through the projects at the end of each chapter. Applying the principles learned in this book is a surefire way to set your district up for a strong financial future."

—**Leslie Scott**, EdD, human resources director for SKC, Inc., former HR
director for Pressley Ridge and Propel Schools, Pittsburgh, Pennsylvania

"What a great relief to have this book, *Making Sense of School Finance*, from my exceptional teacher in graduate school. In-depth knowledge of the intricate workings of school finances is a *conditio sine qua non* for success whether in public or nonpublic domains.

"Though CFOs and accountants have the ball of finances squarely in their court, the general knowledge that Dr. Born has provided in this well-researched book will assuredly arm school administrators, especially in the private sector where the staff is not always ahead of the game in finance matters.

"As a new superintendent of schools in a Catholic Diocese, this book has opened my eyes to the variety of government funding sources open to the nonpublic sector. In digesting the contents of this book, new school administrators like myself will surely develop better competencies regarding financial processes that ensure legal compliance and also guarantee operational efficiency and vitality required of all in schools and central offices."

—**Fr. Isaac Nnanna Ogba**, superintendent of schools,
Roman Catholic Diocese of Gallup, Gallup, New Mexico

# Making Sense
# of School Finance

# Making Sense of School Finance

## A Practical State-by-State Approach

Clinton Born

Published in partnership with the
Association of School Business Officials International (ASBO)

ROWMAN & LITTLEFIELD
Lanham • Boulder • New York • London

Published in partnership with the
Association of School Business Officials International (ASBO)

Published by Rowman & Littlefield
An imprint of The Rowman & Littlefield Publishing Group, Inc.
4501 Forbes Boulevard, Suite 200, Lanham, Maryland 20706
www.rowman.com

6 Tinworth Street, London SE11 5AL, United Kingdom

British Library Cataloguing in Publication Information Available

**Library of Congress Cataloging-in-Publication Data**

Names: Born, Clinton, 1948– author. | Rowman and Littlefield, Inc. | Association of
    School Business Officials International.
Title: Making sense of school finance : a practical state-by-state approach / Clinton Born.
Description: Lanham : Rowman & Littlefield Publishing Group, 2020. | "Published
    in partnership with the Association of School Business Officials International
    (ASBO)" | Includes bibliographical references and index. | Summary: "Making Sense
    of School Finance: A Practical State-by-State Approach thoroughly and clearly
    describes complex school finance concepts regarding local, state, and federal revenue
    along with authentic accounting processes in a straightforward manner for public,
    nonpublic, and charter school leaders"— Provided by publisher.
Identifiers: LCCN 2019056390 (print) | LCCN 2019056391 (ebook) | ISBN
    9781475856651 (Cloth : acid-free paper) | ISBN 9781475856668 (Paperback) | ISBN
    9781475856675 (ePub)
Subjects: LCSH: Education—Finance.
Classification: LCC LB2824 .B65 2020 (print) | LCC LB2824 (ebook) | DDC
    371.2/06—dc23
LC record available at https://lccn.loc.gov/2019056390
LC ebook record available at https://lccn.loc.gov/2019056391

♾™ The paper used in this publication meets the minimum requirements of American
National Standard for Information Sciences—Permanence of Paper for Printed Library
Materials, ANSI/NISO Z39.48-1992.

To my dear, departed parents who inspired my life
accomplishments—Doris I. and Clayton W. Born Sr.—and my
loving wife, Monna Born, who supports my endeavors
and endures my endless hours on the internet and computer

# Contents

# Foreword

For educational leadership students who aspire to positions such as principal and superintendent, Dr. Clinton Born's extraordinarily thorough *Making Sense of School Finance: A Practical State-by-State Approach* is essential reading. I had the fortune of beginning my collaboration with Dr. Born on the editing and formatting of this work through my role at Precision Consulting, and I still recall our first conversation about his visions for the textbook.

Drawing on his robust professional background, Dr. Born explained how his tenure as a school leader, in combination with his current work as an online instructor for educational leadership courses, led him to recognize the need for this particular textbook, and I could see his logic instantly. He noted that in spite of great variation in school finance schemas across states, he had not encountered a textbook that addressed school finance on a state-by-state level.

The value of state-specific information for educational leadership students across the United States is clearly a unique benefit offered by Dr. Born's text, and this becomes more important as online programs in educational leadership increase in prevalence. In any single online course, there might be students from any number of states.

With this text, online instructors and learners now have access to a source of information that covers the broad landscape of school finance in the United States while also providing details that are specific to each state. This provides the opportunity for individualized learning experiences, which Dr. Born locates within a broader national context that allows students to compare and contrast their state's practices with those of other states. Chapter 2 allows the reader to compare and contrast local funding procedures across the states, and chapter 3 allows for such examination of state funding procedures. Chapter 4 brings to light the universalities of U.S. school funding in an examination of federal revenue allocations to schools.

Providing context for these technical discussions, chapter 1 provides an intriguing discussion of the historical development of U.S. school funding since our colonial days. Dr. Born brings out the "story" behind this complex topic, which highlights the fact that school finance today, in all of its complexities and controversialities, is just the current chapter in a continually unfolding story of school officials, U.S. citizens, and lawmakers collaborating toward the shared goal of educating our youth.

Given that funding legislation emerges from and aligns with our diverse perspectives and values as a nation, controversies are inevitable; Dr. Born's note in chapter 1 that many states have pending lawsuits related to funding constitutionality illustrates this point. In the midst of controversy and various calls for reform, however, Dr. Born's perspective is that in-depth understanding of the school finance system as it exists today is essential to educational leaders' performance in their professional roles.

Concluding this text, chapter 5 provides a detailed discussion of accounting practices associated with school budget management and oversight. In line with the preceding chapters, this last chapter covers complex and technical material that occupies a very meaningful place in the story of school finance. Careful and thorough accounting is vital to ensure that districts use these precious resources intended with protections against misuse.

The first four chapters in this volume illustrate the enormity of the social enterprise school finance constitutes, and we citizens all contribute to and benefit from this great social mission in so many ways. Making the best use of the funds that we have is enormously important, and I hope that as you move forward in your career in school administration, Dr. Born's work in this volume inspires in you a sense of pride to safeguard these most valuable resources.

*Sandra Nelms, editor, holds degrees in both English and psychology and is currently pursuing her MBA.*

# Preface

*Making Sense of School Finance: A Practical State-by-State Approach* is a resource for readers in public, nonpublic, and charter school surroundings. Based upon the author's years of school administrative experience, real-world application, and extensive research, this text, rivaled by no other school finance book, thoroughly and clearly describes complicated concepts in a straightforward manner regarding local, state, and federal revenues in addition to authentic accounting processes.

School district finances drive the engine to grant primary and secondary education's successes. Without proper funding, a school will struggle to achieve students' academic successes, and without leaders who comprehend the fundamentals of state-specific school finance revenue, the opportunity for utmost students' achievements falters.

After scanning the market of school finance textbooks, a definite need surfaced to deliver a text that distinctly explains public, nonpublic, and charter school revenue on a state-by-state basis because approximately 80 percent of public school funding derives from distinct state laws and local provisions. In addition, because a void exists in texts on charter school funding by state, including content for this development was unmistakable as educational choice sweeps the country. Having searched for a current nonpublic school funding source for years, a text to address these schools' revenue was evident as well.

Due to the steady emergence of online classes with attending students from any number of states in unique circumstances, a school finance resource that guides readers to content about their particular situation is priceless. The necessity for a state-by-state resource is essential for educational leadership professors to differentiate instruction and impart legitimate information on the nuances of local, state, and federal revenue for public, nonpublic, and charter schools. This five-chapter book affords a decisive format for content delivery in an eight- or ten-week online course. Objectives open each chapter aligned with the National Policy Board for Educational Administration (NPBEA) standards (2018)—*National Educational Leadership Preparation Recognition Standards: Building-Level*. Readers may retrieve these standards at www.npbea.org.

Above all, this comprehensive resource will benefit readers through

- public, nonpublic, and charter school content for each reader's situation;
- authentic, end-of-chapter projects to extend genuine subject matter comprehension;
- illustrated figures for funding allocations and tables to differentiate substance because each topic warrants unique consideration based on the reader's physical location and particular circumstance; and
- references to Ohio funding because the author hails from the Buckeye State.

Enjoy the text and advance your comprehension of local, state, and federal funding unique to your needs.

# Acknowledgments

Please acknowledge my appreciation to several individuals who contributed to the development of this book. I am extremely thankful for Sandra Nelms, editor, who suggested significant writing improvements to the text and dramatically advanced my writing skill. I also value Dr. Katherine E. Calabria, my colleague at Franciscan University of Steubenville, who encouraged me to write this text.

*Chapter One*

# American School Finance Background

## OBJECTIVES

After reading this chapter, you should be able to

✓ reiterate the major events in the history of school finance (NELP 5.3, 6.1, 6,2, 6.3);
✓ confirm and compare a district's percentages of general fund revenue sources and expenditures with national average percentages (NELP 1.2, 6.1, 6.2, 6.3);
✓ identify the school finance fiscal players for a school district (NELP 5.3, 6.1, 6.2, 6.3); and
✓ categorize ethical business dilemmas for school administrators (NELP 2.1. 2.2, 2.3).

Financial support and school funding policies for primary and secondary education have evolved since the Revolutionary War due to changing political views, economic conditions, and societal movements. Legislative actions and litigation outcomes, additionally, have influenced present-day fiscal regulations. Developing political and social happenings, varying tax structures, and changing distribution systems depict the context for understanding how and why education funding progressed over the years.

During America's colonial period in the seventeenth century, educational purposes and beliefs varied by region. The Puritan influence dominated the New England colonies with students studying biblical fundamentals. Sponsored by various religious denominations, schools in the Mid-Atlantic colonies stressed a functional education—boys acquired trade skills and girls learned household duties and social graces. In the Southern colonies, socioeconomic class distinguished schooling; children from poor households received a rudimentary education, while wealthy plantation owners hired private tutors to teach their children reading, writing, spelling, and arithmetic. Although schooling was available for most children in all colonies, governmental subsidies for a formal education were scarce (Hinman, 2012).

The first public school supported by taxes began in 1635 in Dedham, Massachusetts. The Massachusetts Act of 1647 established the state's right to create and maintain elementary schools for every child in small towns; the act further founded "grammar schools" for all youth in larger cities aimed at Harvard preparation, when fitting.

This law marked the inauguration of property tax as a means to finance public education although landowners did not pay the entire cost. To supplement the scant tax, families supported schools by paying tuition, supplying schoolhouse essentials (e.g., wood for heat), or lodging the schoolmaster (Sparkman, 1994).

Although America's founding fathers were supportive of education, the U.S. Constitution neither mandated education for the citizenry nor obligated money for schools. In fact, the U.S. Constitution's Tenth Amendment (U.S. Const. amend. X, 1791) reserved these powers to the states. As years passed, state legislatures performed various education functions by establishing operational structures, allocating budgets, and prescribing funding delivery mechanisms (Alexander & Alexander, 2019).

In the early nineteenth century, American primary schools were mostly under the authority of churches or charities, although wealthy families typically schooled their children at private schools. To establish free schooling in New York City circa 1805, the Public School Society, a committee of the city's prominent citizens, opened public schools for all children. The society raised money through membership dues and philanthropic gifts to operate such schools (Ravich, 2019).

These early schools emphasized Protestant beliefs; Catholic school supporters voiced disapproval and demanded money to sustain their schools. When the Public School Society in 1840 would not fund Catholic schools, disputes erupted. Following the quarrels, the wealthy businessmen of the Public School Society remained staunch in denying funds for Catholic schools because they regarded Protestant beliefs as the "common culture" in the United States (Ravich, 2019).

To cement this principle after the Civil War, legislatures in many states modified constitutions with so-called "baby Blaine amendments" to block public monies for Catholic schools. Senator James G. Blaine of Maine proposed an amendment to the U.S. Constitution in 1874, declaring that tax collected by the government could not fund religious teachings in schools. Although this amendment was defeated in 1875, the tenet, incorporated into 34 state constitutions over the next three decades, prevented Catholic schools from receiving public dollars (Alexander & Alexander, 2019).

As states entered the Union, education clauses in constitutions created free public schools by commanding a "common," "uniform," or "efficient" standard to describe the state's responsibility. To pay for public schools, locally collected property tax was the ordinary revenue source (Alexander & Alexander, 2019). Due to mounting state fiscal obligations, Wisconsin levied the first individual state income tax in 1911 with a portion to finance elementary and secondary public schools (Loughead, Walczak, & Bishop-Henchman, 2019).

A flat grant was the earliest method to disperse state money to schools based on a legislatively fixed per-student allocation. To set state aid for a school district, the flat grant formula divided the number of district students into the legislative per pupil sum (Odden & Picus, 2020).

The foundation program, a distribution method designed in the 1920s and based on fiscal capacity (i.e., ability to raise local property tax), intently ensured uniform state monies for all school districts (Odden & Picus, 2020).

With foundation funding, the state legislature specified a per-student funding level and set a minimum property tax rate applied to a district's property valuation to ascertain fiscal capacity. Using these two variables to establish a district's foundation monies, the state financed the difference between a district's aggregate per-pupil funding amount minus the obligatory local property tax share (Odden & Picus, 2020).

During the 1930s and 1940s, many states began collecting general sales tax to increase state coffers for financing public schools and other state commitments (Mikesell & Kioko, 2018). During this time in a few states, power equalization and full funding models allocated state aid.

After World War II, public aid for parochial schools was back in the news. In *Everson v. Board of Education* (1947), the U.S. Supreme Court ruled that the cost of bus fares to transport parochial children to nonpublic schools was reimbursable to parents with government monies (Alexander & Alexander, 2019).

To compete with the Soviet Union's Sputnik launch in 1957, the U.S. Congress passed the National Defense Education Act (NDEA) of 1958; thereby, altering the national government's stance on education with federal aid allocated to public elementary and secondary schools. The federal government, previously, had not granted dollars for public education except for land grants to build schools and subsidies for vocational education (Congressional Research Service, 2019a).

With the passage of this historic legislation, NDEA specified financial support to improve elementary and secondary public education and opened the gate for future national funding legislation, such as the Richard B. Russell

National School Lunch Act of 1946, Elementary and Secondary Education Act of 1965, and the Education for All Handicapped Children Act of 1975 (Alexander & Alexander, 2019).

To resume the saga regarding parochial school aid from public funds, *Lemon v. Kurtzman* (1971) and *Aguilar v. Felton* (1985) contested the entrenched dogma. In the *Lemon* case, the U.S. Supreme Court found that the practice of using state funds to reimburse private schools for teachers' salaries was unconstitutional. In the *Aguilar v. Felton* case, the High Court first decreed that delivering remedial education to disadvantaged children with federal Title I monies violated the First Amendment's Establishment Clause (Alexander & Alexander, 2019).

In the follow-up *Agostini v. Felton* (1997) case, however, the U.S. Supreme Court overturned the earlier decision and pronounced that public funds could be utilized to educate disadvantaged students in supplemental reading and mathematics instruction at religious schools during regular school hours (Alexander & Alexander, 2019).

During the 1970s, lawsuits challenged state funding distribution methods for primary and secondary public schools. In *Serrano v. Priest* (1971), the California Supreme Court declared that the quality of a child's education should not be subject to residency and associated district wealth (e.g., property values) because uneven fiscal capacities caused huge disparities in basic state aid. In *San Antonio Independent School District v. Rodríguez* (1973), however, the U.S. Supreme Court ruled that Texas's funding system did not violate constitutional equal protection requirements although the Court deemed the system "chaotic and unjust" (Alexander & Alexander, 2019).

The No Child Left Behind Act (2001) and *Zelman v. Simmons-Harris* (2002) advanced children's educational opportunities. The No Child Left Behind Act permitted parents of children in low-performing schools to transfer their children to better-performing schools with state dollars following the child. In *Zelman v. Simmons-Harris*, the U.S. Supreme Court ruled that Ohio's school voucher program did not violate the First Amendment's Establishment Clause, which allowed parents to pay religious, nonpublic school tuition with vouchers funded by the state (Alexander & Alexander, 2019). Presently, 15 states and the District of Columbia have voucher programs for qualifying students (EdChoice, 2019).

School choice flourished in the first two decades of the twenty-first century. A wide array of choices (e.g., interdistrict open enrollment; magnet, virtual, and charter schools; and homeschooling) were available as alternatives to traditional public schools. With the exception of homeschooling, the allotted funds from the state follow the student in the other options.

Opponents argued that publicly funded choice programs harmed public schools by siphoning state monies for these alternatives. Lueken and Shuls (2019) asserted that charter school funding directly decreased state and federal monies to public schools. Forty-four states and the District of Columbia have ratified charter school legislation (Education Commission of the States, 2018b).

Challenges to state Blaine amendments that blocked support for religious schools from public dollars depict school finance conflicts. U.S. appellate courts have mixed results regarding the constitutionality of permitting public assistance for schools sponsored by churches (Alexander & Alexander, 2019).

The Sixth, Eighth, and Tenth Circuits, for instance, overturned discriminatory practices against religious schools receiving public funds; in contrast, the First Circuit and the supreme courts in Vermont and Maine upheld restrictions on public money to parochial schools. Currently, 37 states, sanctioned by Blaine amendments, still prohibit commissioning public funds to religious schools (Dunn, 2018).

The U.S. Supreme Court in 2017 sent the *New Mexico Association of Nonpublic Schools v. Moses*, *Taxpayers for Public Education v. Douglas County School District*, and *Trinity Lutheran Church of Columbia, Inc. v. Comer* cases back to their respective state supreme courts for reconsideration. In *New Mexico Association of Nonpublic Schools v. Moses*, the New Mexico Supreme Court upheld the exclusion of religious and private schools from a state textbook program (Alexander & Alexander, 2019).

In the *Trinity Lutheran* case, the Missouri Supreme Court denied a church-run daycare center from receiving a state grant to replace playground surfaces due to the state's Blaine restriction. Future deliberations by state justice departments may open doors for additional public monies to bolster parochial schools. Nevertheless, until the U.S. Supreme Court definitively resolves this issue, lawmakers and lower courts nationwide will struggle with the uncertainty of approving public monies for private schools (Borders, 2018; Weiner & Green, 2018).

In the *Taxpayers for Public Education* case, the Colorado Supreme Court ruled that the Choice Scholarship Program violated that state's Blaine amendment and barred students from attending religious schools in school choice programs (Alexander & Alexander, 2019). The Colorado Supreme Court in 2018 dismissed the *Taxpayers for Public Education v. Douglas County School District* case as moot at the request of both parties and vacated all previous rulings in the case by the state supreme court and lower benches (Meltzer, 2018).

To fund schools today, 49 states and the District of Columbia authorize local property tax, the largest local revenue source for schools. Forty-one states currently assess individual state income tax on salary and wages to fund public schools and other state responsibilities. New Hampshire and Tennessee tax interest and dividend income only; seven states (Alaska, Florida, Nevada, South Dakota, Texas, Washington, and Wyoming) do not levy a state income tax (Brimley, Verstegen, & Knoeppel, 2020). Five states (Alaska, Delaware, Montana, New Hampshire, and Oregon) do not collect a state general sales tax (Cammenga, 2019).

Regarding fund distribution systems, 32 states and the District of Columbia currently execute some derivation of the foundation model. Nine states (California, Georgia, Kentucky, Louisiana, Montana, New York, Oklahoma, Texas, and Utah) presently utilize a hybrid of models to allocate state funds. Seven states (Arizona, Delaware, Florida, Illinois, Michigan, Vermont, and Wisconsin) employ the power equalization model. Hawaii exercises the full funding model, and North Carolina implements a modified flat grant model (Verstegen, 2018).

Numerous state basic aid formula changes occurred over the years due to legislative actions and court challenges. Most school funding legal challenges contested state allocations either on equity or adequacy grounds. Equity lawsuits asserted that each public primary and secondary child in the state should be entitled to the same education funding level (i.e., local and state) regardless of residency. Adequacy suits alleged that the state legislature failed to deliver an adequate funding level for all districts to meet student academic standards adopted by the state (Alexander & Alexander, 2019).

Since 1973, plaintiffs in 36 states constitutionality opposed the funding method on equity grounds, and 37 states disputed systems on adequacy complaints. At present, six states (Illinois, Massachusetts, New Hampshire, Pennsylvania, Tennessee, and Vermont) have a pending lawsuit or await an appeal decision. Delaware, Hawaii, Mississippi, Nevada, and Utah have not litigated their state funding structure (SchoolFunding.Info, 2019). Because school finance lawsuits are so dynamic, keeping abreast of court decisions and legislative acts is critical for educators and interested parties.

## PUBLIC EDUCATION—BIG BUSINESS

Elementary and secondary public education holds a hefty business influence in the United States with a substantial investment from local communities, state governments, and the federal system. School leaders and the community should realize the impact education has on the nation's economy by recognizing each level of governmental contribution and acknowledging district expenditures.

According to the U.S. Census Bureau (2019a), the total elementary and secondary public education revenue in the United States was $694.1 billion during the 2017 fiscal year, which is the most current Census Bureau data at the time of this publication. State and local governments supplied the majority of elementary and secondary public education dollars. Local sources financed 45.4 percent of the total revenue, state governments supplied 47.3 percent; and the federal government granted 7.3 percent during the 2019 year (National Education Association, 2019b).

Other sources—corporate, private, and foundation grants; federal and state governmental discretionary programs; and fundraisers—provided minimal funding (Bivin et al., 2018). During the past decade, local and state revenue percentages for public education gradually increased; whereas, federal percentages steadily decreased (McFarland et al., 2019). To illustrate trends, table 1.1 shows the percentages of federal, state, and local funding in selected years.

On a national basis, the entire revenue from local sources was $311.7 billion in the 2017 fiscal year, which is the most current Census Bureau data compiled at the time of publication (U.S. Census Bureau, 2019a). Property tax generated 81 percent of the entire local district funding. The remaining 19 percent of all the dollars originated from a variety of other local taxing sources (e.g., sales, income, and miscellaneous) and nontax means. Sales and individual income tax produced the most state monies for elementary and secondary public schools (Snyder, de Brey, & Dillow, 2019).

Each state legislature controls the amount of state funds allotted to each school district and the distribution mechanism. The total revenue for schools from state sources in the United States was $327 billion in the 2017 fiscal year (U.S. Census, 2019a).

Federal funding assists states and schools in an effort to supplement—not supplant—state and local support. The U.S. Department of Education distributes federal monies through a variety of laws and programs approved by the U.S. Congress. States typically apply to the U.S. Department of Education for these funds. After submitting the application and receiving the block

**Table 1.1. Federal, State, and Local Revenue Percentages, 2014–2019[a]**

| School Year | Federal | State | Local |
|---|---|---|---|
| 2014–15 | 8.4% | 46.7% | 45.0% |
| 2015–16 | 8.0% | 47.1% | 44.8% |
| 2016–17 | 7.9% | 47.0% | 45.1% |
| 2017–18 | 7.5% | 47.1% | 45.4% |
| 2018–19 | 7.3% | 47.3% | 45.4% |

*Sources:* National Education Association (2019b) and Snyder et al. (2019).
*Note:* [a]The sum of federal, state, and local revenue percentages may not total 100% because of rounding.

funding, the state department of education reassigns the dollars to local school districts. The annual revenue from federal sources was $55.3 billion in the 2017 fiscal year (U.S. Census, 2019a).

When federal, state, and local revenue sources do not provide sufficient money to fund special projects, schools seek money through other sources, such as discretionary grants from the federal and state governments; corporate, private, and philanthropic endowments; donations; and fundraisers (Bivin et al., 2018).

Elementary and secondary school systems in the United States spent $694.2 billion on education during the 2017 fiscal year, which is the most current Census Bureau data at the time of this publication (U.S. Census Bureau, 2019a). Salaries were the largest district expenditure; employee benefits constituted the second largest expense. Contract costs for utilities, technology maintenance, legal counsel, and insurances represented purchased services from suppliers. Supplies consisted of books and materials for students and teachers (Snyder et al., 2019).

Capital outlay referred to district expenditures for construction and renovation of buildings, purchases of equipment and land, and building leases. Interest on debt pertained to payments from borrowing monies for building construction and other projects (Snyder et al., 2019). Table 1.2 illustrates the expenditures by function spent in the United States and the percentage of total spending per function during fiscal year 2017.

The school-age population in the United States reveals another statistic to capture primary and secondary public education's significance on a grand scale. Actual and projected enrollments lend assistance in projecting future funding, prospective expenditures, and potential resources, including staffing.

According to the most recent U.S. Department of Education data at the time of publication, 50.6 million students in the United States attended kindergarten through grade 12 at traditional public schools, 5.8 million students attended nonpublic institutions, and 3.0 million attended public charter schools in the 2016–2017 school year. Public school enrollment in the United

**Table 1.2.   Expenditures and Percentages by Function, 2017[a]**

| Function | Total Spent | Percentage of Total |
|---|---|---|
| Salaries | $339.7 Billion | 57% |
| Employee Benefits | $136.8 Billion | 23% |
| Purchased Services | $64.6 Billion | 11% |
| Supplies | $43.7 Billion | 7% |
| Other Expenses | $15.2 Billion | 2% |

*Source:* Snyder et al. (2019).
*Note:* [a]Data in the table are the most current compiled by the U.S. Department of Education at the time of publication.

States projects to increase at 2 percent each year through 2028. By 2028, 51.4 million children will be attending public schools in the United States if this projection stays accurate (McFarland et al., 2019).

For future reference, elementary and secondary nonpublic schools are educational institutions with minimal support from public funds or resources. As per McFarland et al. (2019), the nonpublic category considers Catholic schools (e.g., parochial, diocesan, and private), other religious institutions (e.g., Christian, unrestricted specific denomination, and unaffiliated with any denomination), and nonsectarian schools (i.e., no religious affiliation).

Homeschooling, another primary and secondary education alternative, signifies the instruction of school-aged children (i.e., 5–17 years of age) in grades kindergarten through grade 12 at home for most of the day or all day rather than at a public or nonpublic school. Parents who homeschool their children generally do not receive any public aid; however, when a homeschool student participates in a dual enrollment program with a public school, the district usually receives a portion of the state funding (Home School Legal Defense Association, 2019). Annual homeschool enrollments remain inexact because the U.S. Department of Education does not collect these data; however, Ray (2019) reported an estimated 2.3 million children participated in homeschooling during 2016, which is the most current data. Table 1.3 shows actual and projected school-age student enrollment in the United States by school type.

**Table 1.3.  Actual and Projected K–12 Student Enrollment in Millions by School Type[a]**

| Year | Traditional Public | Nonpublic | Public Charter |
|------|--------------------|-----------|----------------|
| 2014–15 | 50.4 | 5.5 | 2.8 |
| 2015–16 | 50.6 | 5.7 | 2.8 |
| 2016–17 | 50.6 | 5.8 | 3.0 |
| 2017–18 | 50.7[b] | 5.9[b] | Not Projected |
| 2018–19 | 50.8[b] | Not Projected | Not Projected |
| 2019–20 | 50.9[b] | Not Projected | Not Projected |
| 2027–28 | 51.4[b] | Not Projected | Not Projected |

*Sources*: McFarland et al. (2019) and Snyder et al. (2019).
*Notes*. [a]Data in the table are the most current compiled by the U.S. Department of Education at the time of publication.
[b]Projected.

## THE FISCAL PLAYERS

To acquire an understanding of school finance, school leaders must be knowledgeable about those parties (i.e., fiscal players) involved in district financial processes and recognize that each person has a distinct role. Because the federal government subsidizes district funding, numerous people at that level influence monetary decisions. Various individuals in the local and state government affect district fiscal dynamics too.

With regard to federal funding for schools, the president of the United States, supported by the Office of Management and Budget staff, announces the preliminary federal budget after consultation with federal agencies, including the Department of Education. With this initial request, the U.S. Congress realizes the recommended fiscal agenda from the president, including spending allocations for public education entitlements and discretionary programs (Center on Budget and Policy Priorities, 2019a).

After the presidential recommendation, members of the U.S. Congress hold hearings to discuss the president's proposal in the House and Senate. House and Senate budget committees separately draft budget proposals. After each motion passes the House and Senate respectively, a joint House and Senate conference committee convenes to resolve disparities. Upon a settlement of differences, both houses adopt the collaborative bill and pass concurrent declarations. Upon passage, Congress sends the bill to the president for final approval (Center on Budget and Policy Priorities, 2019a).

To establish the state education budget, most states follow a similar process as the federal government's budgetary procedures except the governor and state Office of Budget and Management release the initial request. This proposal signifies to members of the state legislature allotments for primary and secondary public education basic and categorical aid along with funding for discretionary programs. State legislators, in turn, develop and adopt a state budget bill that the governor must sign before the act becomes law (National Association of State Budget Officers, 2015). (Note: This source is the foremost reference for state budget officers and others interested in the operation of state governments. According to a National Association of State Budget Officers official, an updated report is published every 5 years with a new edition scheduled for 2020.)

After the governor's approval, the education funds become available to the state department of education under the direction of the state's chief executive officer who oversees the distribution to school districts. The state department of revenue or taxation division collects specific taxes owed to the school district and accordingly distributes these funds (National Association of State Budget Officers, 2015).

The auditor in 41 states and the District of Columbia directs his or her respective jurisdiction's accounting and financial functions. Auditors act as watchdogs over school district fiscal activities, perform governmental audits, and investigate fraud allegations. Connecticut, Florida, Illinois, Maryland, New Jersey, New York, Pennsylvania, Tennessee, and Texas do not have an auditor; the state comptroller in these states executes similar duties as the state auditor (Ballotpedia, 2019a).

Local government officials perform various roles in school finance, especially property tax administration. Although each state may have different titles for officeholders, officials hold similar responsibilities regarding school funding. The Office of the Assessor (2019) in Sacramento and the County Commissioners Association of Ohio (2019) proclaimed that locally elected officials assume the following duties:

- The tax assessor (i.e., appraiser) locates and classifies all the taxable real and personal property within the region, identifies the property owners, defines the assessed value for each property, and verifies appraisals.
- The auditor calculates tax rates, serves as the state's agent for property appraisal, and applies tax reduction factors on tax bills. The auditor also certifies tax referendums to the voters, validates millage rates, and calculates generated income. In regions without a tax assessor, the auditor locates and classifies taxable property.
- The treasurer (i.e., tax collector) collects property tax, calculates and issues property tax bills, and detects as well as assigns the penalties on late payments.
- The board of equalization (i.e., board of revision) often consists of a county commissioner, auditor, assessor, and treasurer. This panel hears individual complaints on property valuations, classifications, and appraisals.
- The county budget commission in Ohio assures that voted tax levies are necessary and in accord with the tax budgets submitted by the school district. This commission includes the county's auditor, treasurer, and prosecuting attorney.

School board members or trustees, as titled in some states, have numerous responsibilities, but the most imperative is district fiscal oversight. Although the school board delegates the responsibility of developing and maintaining the district's fiscal documents (e.g., budget, appropriation, and fiscal reports) to the superintendent and school treasurer/chief fiscal officer (CFO), the board monitors district finances and expenditures on a continual basis. The board also officially approves the district budget, appropriation, revenue, expenditures, and tax rates (Texas Education Agency, 2019a).

The superintendent of schools is the district's chief executive officer who maintains full responsibility for the organization's management and operations, including all functions related to business and fiscal endeavors. Specific financial duties involve negotiating and recommending contracts; creating and monitoring financial documents; approving purchases of materials, supplies, and equipment; overseeing building construction and renovation projects; and supervising staff (Texas Education Agency, 2019a).

The CFO/treasurer (i.e., school business administrator) occupies another high-ranking district position. He or she generally works directly for the school board in concert with the superintendent. The CFO/treasurer creates, recommends, and monitors the district budget and appropriation; prepares financial reports for the board, staff, and community; monitors revenue and expenditures; manages the district's cash flow; deposits monies; coauthorizes purchases; establishes and reconciles accounts; projects fiscal forecasts; pays obligations; and maintains inventories.

Assistant superintendents, school business managers, supervisors, program coordinators, and principals stand responsible for the oversight and control of the daily financial activities in areas under their supervision. These school officials should monitor expenditures and scrutinize purchases. Teachers and staff members become directly associated with the financial resources of the district treasury by expending funds.

The residents within a school district exhibit a major role in funding schools. First, citizens pay federal income tax, which obligates the federal portion of the school budget. Local residents also pay state income and sales tax, which backs public schools through the state funding system. Property owners pay a real estate tax, and the electorate in many states decides the success or failure of a levy or bond issue. The dollars received by a school district, consequently, is greatly dependent on community individuals.

## ETHICAL CONSIDERATIONS

School administrators face ethical situations and dilemmas daily, especially in handling public money and transacting school business. A school official with fiduciary obligations must safeguard district assets, accurately prepare documents and reports, and properly collect and expend school funds to ensure principled district operations. In doing so, school administrators must function at the highest legal, ethical, and moral standards. Administrative decisions, founded on a code of ethics, become paramount (AASA, The School Superintendents Association, 2019a).

AASA, the School Superintendents Association (2019a) described characteristics and values regarding ethical business behavior. Supported by AASA, the School Superintendents Association tenets, ethical school administrators

- abide by appropriate state, federal, and constitutional laws plus school board policies;

- remain honest and truthful in all business transactions without misleading or deceiving others;
- maintain fiscal integrity through meticulous account monitoring, accurate revenue projecting, and watchful purchasing in pursuit of the best products and services at reasonable prices;
- act with professional reason, fairness, and impartiality in every business activity without arbitrarily exercising power or gaining advantage of others;
- acknowledge and accept personal accountability for all decisions using prudence and rationale judgment; and
- exhibit transparency through actions that impart confidence to the community, stakeholders, and staff.

In handling public monies and managing projects, Locatelli, Mariani, Sainati, and Greco (2017) described the following unethical school leader conduct:

- Abuse of power arises when an individual in authority exerts his/her position to obtain a personal benefit. For instance, a staff member who asks a school custodian to strip, wax, and buff the floors in his/her home is abusing power.
- Accepting personal gifts of substantial value is unethical when given by a vendor to influence a school official's action. For example, a school official who attends a vacation paid by a company at an exclusive resort in exchange for future purchases from the firm offering the vacation is unprincipled.
- Conflict of interest occurs when the personal interests of a school official are, or appear to be, at odds with the school district's best interests as a whole. For example, when the principal buys overpriced shirts for honor roll students from a relative, this deed characterizes a conflict of interest, an unethical act.
- Falsifying records involve altering, changing, or modifying a document to deceive others. A record falsification occurs when a school administrator inappropriately inflates the number of attending special education students, with the purpose of increasing funding. Audits usually uncover the illegal act of changing records.
- Fraud happens when an individual deliberately deceives or unjustly tricks others in order to gain money, property, or services. For example, an administrator who grants an employee credit for unworked overtime hours commits fraud.
- Misappropriation of public funds or property refers to an instance when spending school funds for unapproved purposes. Laws require school funds and property be sourced only for activities associated with the performance of public duties and not for private gain. A misappropriation develops when a school employee uses a school vehicle for personal transportation. This

misuse is not exactly theft because the school official did not actually steal the transport; however, this situation abuses the intended purpose for the school vehicle.
- Theft of public monies or property by school officials ranges from minor misdeeds (e.g., bringing office supplies home) to felony offenses, such as embezzlement (e.g., stealing money from the public treasury).

Unethical actions, unfortunately, occur too frequently in schools. To protect the district and public from malfeasance, a fidelity bond, required by law for certain public officials, guarantees the faithful performance of duties in properly managing and handling all district funds. Depending on the misdeed, the consequences for unethical behavior may include embarrassment, suspension, job termination, or criminal penalties. Educational leaders should ground all financial decisions on ethical practices. The public and district stakeholders highly regard the moral and ethical fabric of administrative decisions and hold officials accountable for their choices; thus, school leaders must remain steadfastly vigilant about their actions.

## SUMMARY

American school finance evolved over centuries to its current standpoint with reliance on local and state tax. Political policies and social movements influenced the evolution of school finance principles. State and federal laws associated with school finance, funding sources, and distribution methods are key facets in the transformation of actions to the present status.

Elementary and secondary public education is an enormous enterprise in the United States. Every year, local, state, federal, and grant sources supply billions of dollars to educate children. Salaries, employee benefits, purchased services, supplies, capital outlay, and interest on debt account for the billions spent. Numerous contributors define a school district's funding; others administer, monitor, and oversee school finances.

When administering public money and participating in business transactions, school officials must remain steadfast in their ethical performance; otherwise, they will find themselves in legal trouble.

## PROJECTS

1. Discover and report, by source, your school district's revenue percentages and compare the discoveries with the national averages (see table 1.1).

2. Find and recount, by function, your school district's annual expenditure percentages and compare the findings with the national averages (see table 2.2).
3. Count and report the number of students attending traditional public, nonpublic (i.e., religiously associated and nonsectarian), and charter schools in addition to homeschooled children in your residential area.
4. Identify and state the fiscal players for your district by name, position title, and duty.
5. Discuss the following ethical dilemmas with colleagues:
   a. You won a big-screen television at the state school board association conference. Your school board paid for your registration, lodging, meals, and travel. What are the ethical considerations in this scenario? What would you do in this situation with the big-screen television?
   b. The school district needs to pave parking lots, which is a $200,000 expense. A close relative owns a paving company. What are the ethical considerations in this scenario? How will you handle this situation in deciding who will pave the lots?
   c. You have heard that a teacher under your charge has falsified a travel expense account. What are the ethical considerations in this scenario? How will you manage this situation with the employee?

*Chapter Two*

# Local Revenue

## OBJECTIVES

After reading this chapter, you should be able to

✓ distinguish the different types of school districts (NELP 6.3);
✓ understand a school district's local revenue sources and discriminate between the unique processes for each by state (NELP 3.2, 5.3, 6.1, 6.2, 6.3);
✓ explain terminology related to local revenue (NELP 5.3, 6.1, 6.2, 6.3); and
✓ examine a school budget and identify local revenue sources (NELP 6.1. 6.2, 6.3).

The Tenth Amendment to the U.S. Constitution (U.S. Const. amend. X, 1791) reserves the power of states to devise and implement taxation systems along with the authority to regulate and control public education. As states entered the Union, each state's respective constitution stipulated commitments for primary and secondary public education (Alexander & Alexander, 2019). The U.S. Census Bureau (2019b) reported 31 states with independent school districts as local governmental subdivisions. This type of district maintains legal jurisdiction to levy tax rates within state regulations and statutory limits, accept revenue, prepare budgets, and authorize expenditures.

By contrast, four states and the District of Columbia formed dependent school districts with a parent government (e.g., state, municipality, county, borough, township, or town) authorized as the legal authority to levy tax rates, receive taxes, and approve final budgets. Further, 15 states sanctioned a mixture of independent and dependent school districts (U.S. Census Bureau, 2019b). Table 2.1 shows the entire number of elementary and secondary public school districts, by type, for each state and the District of Columbia (i.e., jurisdictions).

**Table 2.1.   Number of Public School Districts by Governing Type(s)**

| Jurisdiction | Independent Districts | Dependent Districts | Jurisdiction | Independent Districts | Dependent Districts |
|---|---|---|---|---|---|
| Alabama | 137 | | Nebraska | 269 | |
| Alaska | | 55 | Nevada | 17 | |
| Arizona | 242 | 12 | New Hampshire | 168 | 10 |
| Arkansas | 235 | | New Jersey | 519 | 74 |
| California | 1011 | 57 | New Mexico | 96 | |
| Colorado | 180 | | New York | 678 | 36 |
| Connecticut | 17 | 149 | North Carolina | | 174 |
| Delaware | 19 | | North Dakota | 179 | |
| Florida | 95 | | Ohio | 666 | |
| Georgia | 180 | | Oklahoma | 542 | |
| Hawaii | | 1 | Oregon | 230 | |
| Idaho | 118 | | Pennsylvania | 514 | |
| Illinois | 886 | | Rhode Island | 4 | 32 |
| Indiana | 289 | | South Carolina | 81 | |
| Iowa | 348 | | South Dakota | 150 | |
| Kansas | 306 | | Tennessee | 14 | 128 |
| Kentucky | 173 | | Texas | 1073 | 2 |
| Louisiana | 69 | 1 | Utah | 41 | |
| Maine | 98 | 160 | Vermont | 277 | |
| Maryland | | 39 | Virginia | 1 | 133 |
| Massachusetts | 85 | 236 | Washington | 295 | |
| Michigan | 571 | | Washington, DC | | 2 |
| Minnesota | 333 | | West Virginia | 55 | |
| Mississippi | 157 | 3 | Wisconsin | 438 | 3 |
| Missouri | 430 | | Wyoming | 55 | |
| Montana | 313 | | | | |

*Source:* U.S. Census Bureau (2019b).

Varying local tax and nontax sources generate income for public school districts in the United States. Local sources financed 45.4 percent of the total revenue during the 2018–2019 year (National Education Association, 2019b).

The National Center for Education Statistics, in conjunction with the U.S. Census Bureau, gathers local school revenue data on an annual basis with *Form F-33: Annual Survey of Local Government Finances* (U.S. Census Bureau, 2019c). School districts reported local unrestricted revenue sources— monies not dedicated to a specific purpose and expended for any intent. Property tax was the foremost unrestricted local income stream for districts (McFarland et al., 2019).

Other local revenue sources reported on the *F-33* included tax on general sales or gross receipts, individual and corporate income, public utilities, and other miscellaneous duties; nontax revenue was another source. Nontax revenues on the *F-33* encompassed tuition, transportation fees, textbook sales and rentals, school lunch purchases, district activity receipts, service income, royalties, facility rentals, property transactions, investment earnings, fines, private contributions, and student fees (U.S. Census Bureau, 2019c).

Table 2.2 presents the average revenue percentages of property tax and other sources as portions of the total local income for all public school systems in the United States from 2013 to 2017, which illustrates the most current data compiled by the U.S. Department of Education at the time of publication.

**Table 2.2.   Average Local Revenue Percentages in the United States, 2013–17[a]**

| School Year | Property Tax | Other Local Revenue Sources |
| --- | --- | --- |
| 2012–13 | 80.8% | 19.2% |
| 2013–14 | 80.9% | 19.1% |
| 2014–15 | 81.0% | 19.0% |
| 2015–16 | 81.2% | 18.8% |
| 2016–17 | 81.4% | 18.6% |

*Source:* U.S. Department of Education (2019a).
*Note:* [a]Data in the table are the most current compiled by the U.S. Department of Education at the time of publication.

## PROPERTY TAX

Property tax in 49 states and the District of Columbia funds many local public services, including elementary and secondary public education. Hawaii does not permit local property tax collection for schools. Property taxing government subdivisions include independent school districts, municipalities, counties, townships, and special purpose districts. Police, fire, sanitation, and water departments; airports; cemeteries; conservation divisions; libraries; health and social service agencies; parks; and transit authorities comprise special purpose taxing districts. Taxing subdivisions may overlap, meaning a taxpayer may pay property tax to more than one subdivision (Brien, 2018).

During the nineteenth century in the United States, local property tax was the sole income for schools; states began to contribute in the 1920s. Property tax typifies an ad valorem tax because the duty represents a percentage of a property's value. Most property tax originates from real property (Brimley et al., 2020).

Compared to real property, personal property typically comprises a relatively small share of the locally assessed property, although 42 states and the District of Columbia permit tolls on some kind of tangible personal property. Four states authorize property tax on intangible personal property (Lincoln Institute of Land Policy, 2018).

## Property Classification

Property classification distinguishes property groupings with common characteristics for tax purposes. Although each state acknowledges specific property classifications by statute, three universal classes across the country may be subject to property tax—real, tangible personal, and intangible personal. A number of distinct kinds of property are tax-exempt (Lincoln Institute of Land Policy, 2018).

Real property refers to permanent buildings, structures, and land. Residential, commercial, agricultural, and utilities along with industrial properties characterize customary categories. All states and the District of Columbia sanction tax on real property owned by an individual, business, or utility company (Lincoln Institute of Land Policy, 2018).

Tangible personal property denotes physical property permanently unattached to land, such as business inventory, furniture, equipment, machinery, motor vehicles, aircraft, and watercraft. Thirty-five states and the District of Columbia tax business equipment and machinery, 12 states tax motor vehicles as personal property, and 11 states tax business inventory. Eight states eliminated tangible personal property tax (Lincoln Institute of Land Policy, 2018).

To view tangible personal property assessments for a specific state, click or search for the Lincoln Institute of Land Policy website address at https://www .lincolninst.edu/research-data/data-toolkits/significant-features-property -tax/access-property-tax-database/property-tax-in-detail, select a state and year, and click taxable personal property.

Intangible personal property pertains to nonphysical property—stocks, bonds, copyrights, and trademarks. Arizona, Georgia, Minnesota, and Tennessee tax intangible personal property (Lincoln Institute of Land Policy, 2018).

Exempt property signifies untaxed real property, usually consisting of government property; religious and charitable holdings; health care facilities; literary institutions; and cemeteries. Although all states exempt specific property types by statute, states differ regarding the particular exemptions (Lincoln Institute of Land Policy, 2018).

To view the exempt property types for a specific state, click or search for the Lincoln Institute of Land Policy website at https://www.lincolninst.edu/research -data/data-toolkits/significant-features-property-tax/access-property-tax-data base/property-tax-in-detail, select a state and year, and click exempt property.

## Property Valuation and Assessment Ratio

A property's true or fair market value refers to the price that an informed, ready buyer would pay a willing seller on the open market. To establish a property's fair market value, assessors examine selling prices and compare property sales among similar properties (Appraisal Foundation, 2019).

An assessment ratio, regulated by state statute and established by property classification, sets the percentage of a property's fair market value subject to taxation. Assessment ratios across the United States vary widely by state, and percentages may differ by property class within a state. Delaware, New York, Oklahoma, Pennsylvania, Rhode Island, and Virginia do not have a uniform statewide statutory assessment ratio (Lincoln Institute of Land Policy, 2018).

In states without a statewide assessment ratio, local government officials approve the assessment ratio for their locality. For instance, Delaware's assessment percentages contrast in three counties—New Castle County, 100 percent of a property's true market value; Kent County, 60 percent; and Sussex County, 50 percent (Lincoln Institute of Land Policy, 2018).

A district's aggregate property valuation represents the value of all real property within a school district. Valuation per pupil, a particularly useful element in many state basic aid formulas to compare districts and equalize aid, illustrates the wealth of a school district. A district's per pupil property wealth signifies a community's affluence (i.e., assessed or actual property values) to support education. Dividing a district's student enrollment into the district's aggregate valuation calculates the valuation per pupil. All states, except Pennsylvania, employ property values in some part of the basic aid measurement for a district's fiscal capacity (Verstegen, 2018).

To see property classifications with assessment ratios for a specific state, click or search for the Lincoln Institute of Land Policy website at https:// www.lincolninst.edu/classification/with your state.

To calculate the assessed value or taxable value for a property, tax specialists multiply the fair market value by the established assessment ratio. Therefore, the assessed value computation for a $100,000 home (i.e., fair market value) with a 35 percent assessment ratio equals a $35,000 assessed value.

## Appraisal and Reappraisal

An individual appraisal represents an assessor's opinion of a single property's value. A mass appraisal, aimed at property tax, establishes classifications and fair market values for all property in a given area. Because mass reappraisal cycles vary by state law, each state maintains an established procedure with mass reappraisals periodically conducted in sections of the state rather than statewide (Lincoln Institute of Land Policy, 2018).

The Appraisal Foundation (2019) reported that most states utilized the *Uniform Standards of Professional Appraisal Practice*. Using these standards to set a property's fair market value, an appraiser (i.e., assessor) examines one of three indicators—market sales, replacement cost, or property income.

The market sales approach to determine the fair market value, the most common strategy for residential houses, compares the selling price of similar houses with respect to location, size, condition, and sale date. The replacement cost approach estimates a building's restoration price after subtracting depreciation to resolve the fair market value. The income approach approximates an apartment, store, or factory's income for the fair market value (Appraisal Foundation, 2019).

A property owner in each state holds the right to challenge the appraisal value, after receiving the determination. Each state institutes procedures to appeal an appraisal. The county board of equalization in many states may adjust the fair market value of the disputed property upon validated reasons from the owner (Appraisal Foundation, 2019).

To view the revaluation cycle for a specific state, click or search for the Lincoln Institute of Land Policy website at https://www.lincolninst.edu/research-data/data-toolkits/significant-features-property-tax/access-property-tax-database/property-tax-in-detail, select a state and year, and click assessment administration.

## Millage Rate

To receive real estate property tax in most states, a district assesses a millage rate on each property's assessed value for the tax year. The property tax rate (i.e., millage) represents the factor applied to the assessed property value to calculate property tax liability. Millage rates, expressed in mills, equal one-tenth of one cent (.001); therefore, one mill equates to $1,000 of property value. A district millage rate, approved by an affirmative residential vote in most states, remains consistent within a school district; however, millage rates vary by district across the state.

After defining the assessed value for a property and certifying millage rates, the tax authority computes each property owner's tax obligation. The property tax duty on a $100,000 (i.e., fair market value) home with a 35 percent assessment ratio equals a $35,000 assessed value. Thus, when a property's assessed value is $35,000 with a 15 (.015) millage rate, the tax obligation equals $525. A 5 mill (.005) tax increase obliges the taxpayer an additional $175, totaling $700 before applying exemptions, which will be clarified later in the chapter.

A few states (e.g., California) define property tax rates and increases by a percentage of the property's assessment value rather than millage to simplify explanations. By reporting property tax rates as a percentage, property, income, and sales tax hold a uniform unit (i.e., percentage) for easier comparisons (Odden & Picus, 2020).

When a district requests additional money with this configuration, the school system conveys the need as a percentage. For instance, when a school system's tax rate is 1.5 percent on a house with a $35,000 assessed value, the tax commitment would be $525, equaling the same amount as the millage example. This calculation represents a 1.5 percent (.015) tax rate multiplied by the $35,000 assessed value. When the district needs a .5 percent tax rate raise, the increase would be .5 percent (.005) multiplied by the $35,000 assessed value, representing a $175 tax increase. The total 2 percent (.02) tax responsibility will be $700 before deducting any exemptions.

A district's property tax base (i.e., aggregate assessed value) designates the sum of all taxable property values in the school system. To calculate a district's property tax yield (i.e., total property tax collection), tax authorities multiply the tax base by the millage rate (Brimley et al., 2020). The property tax yield for Pennsylvania's Neshaminy School District was $120,414,804 based on a $7,922,026,578 assessed value with a 15.2 (.0152) millage rate (see appendix-exhibit 1).

The Ohio School Boards Association (2018) labeled three types of millage rates—inside, outside, and effective millage. Inside millage (i.e., unvoted millage) refers to levied millage permitted by law without voter consent. Ohio law, for example, allows local government subdivisions (e.g., townships and school districts) to share 10 mills without voter approval. Ohio school districts typically collect less than 5 inside mills of the allowable 10 mills. Rates may differ by township within a school district.

Outside millage (i.e., voted millage) denotes millage approved by resident voters in addition to the inside millage. For instance, 5 inside mills with 45 outside mills equals 50 aggregate mills. A levy referendum is often required to increase outside millage.

Ohio's effective millage or collected millage means the levied tax rate after applying adjustments due to a mass appraisal. Ohio House Bill 920 (33 Ohio Rev. Code §319.301) limits the revenue from voted millage on a renewal levy after reappraisals to the same income as the initial levy (Ohio School Boards Association, 2018). Thus, when a district's tax base (i.e., assessed valuation) rises after a reappraisal, the millage rate reduces to yield the exact same dollars the voters initially approved.

For example, on an initial 45 mills sanctioned by the district, a district property tax yield is $2,250,000 on a $50,000,000 aggregate assessed valuation. When a district's assessed valuation rises from $50,000,000 to $60,000,000 after a mass reappraisal, the effective millage rate reduces to 37.5 mills due to HB 920 and holds the district tax yield to the same $2,250,000 from the initial levy.

The effective millage rate is essential to calculate a taxpayer's property tax obligation. For instance, when a homeowner in Ohio owns a $100,000 house (i.e., fair market value) with a $35,000 assessed value and the district collects 45 effective mills, the taxable amount is $1,575. When a taxpayer's assessed value rises to $105,000 after an adjusted reappraisal, the district's aggregate property tax collection remains the same due to HB 920. Thereby, the effective millage rate lowers to 37.5 mills, and the property owner's tax obligation reduces to $1,378.13. Although there are adjustments on every single parcel and additional taxes from new structures in the district, the district collects the same tax yield as before the appraisal.

Even though tax authorities compute a district's aggregate assessed valuation and property tax yield along with taxpayers' obligations, wise school leaders comprehend these computations to explain the calculations to district property owners and stakeholders.

## Referendums

When a district wants to collect property tax above statutory limits, state law considers three types of referendums—operating and permanent improvement levies in many states along with bond issues (Ohio School Boards Association, 2018). With voter approval in most states, an excess operating levy referendum grants additional money for any expenditure within a school budget. Bond referendums, often called bond issues, and permanent improvement levies in many states exclusively raise funds for nonoperating expenses or capital expenditures (e.g., new school construction, building renovation, buses, equipment, and other fixed assets). This chapter solely considers operating levies.

Thirty-three states (see table 2.3) require voter approval for school districts to boost operating millage above statutory limits (Ballotpedia, 2019b; Lincoln Institute of Land Policy, 2018). Ohio school district residents, for instance, may approve varying types of operating levies—limited (1 to 5 years), emergency to avoid an operating debt (1 to 5 years), continuing (indefinite), or a renewal after the expiration of a limited or emergency levy (Ohio School Boards Association, 2018).

A local referendum is unnecessary in particular states. Based upon a school's budget request, a majority vote by the tax jurisdiction's committee members (boroughs, Alaska; county or city councils, Maryland, Tennessee, and the District of Columbia; and local school boards, Arizona, South Dakota, and Texas) sets the millage tax rate (Ballotpedia, 2019b).

The community residents in Connecticut, Maine, New Hampshire, New York, Rhode Island, and Vermont must approve a district's annual school budget, which sets the millage rate (Ballotpedia, 2019b). To compute the necessary millage rate for a requested budget, tax authorities and school officials divide the requested budget amount into the district's property tax base. For example, an $800 million aggregate district assessed valuation with a $25 million budget requires a 31.25 millage rate.

Because dependent school districts in Massachusetts, North Carolina, and Virginia do not have taxing authority, the parent government (e.g., municipal council in Massachusetts and county board of commissioners in North Carolina and Virginia) proposes property tax increases in excess operating levy referendums (Ballotpedia, 2019b). The state of Hawaii acts as the property taxing authority for schools because a state statute does not permit local property tax.

Kentucky has a complex set of procedures to increase property tax. In Kentucky, the board of education does not have the authority to levy a tax more than the revenue produced in excess of a 4 percent increase over the prior year without the action subject to a recall election. When a school district proposes such an increase in revenue from existing property of more than 4 percent, the portion of the rate exceeding 4 percent growth is subject to voter recall through a referendum process (Lincoln Institute of Land Policy, 2018).

School districts in Georgia and Louisiana may solicit voter authorization for a local sales tax levy in addition to a property tax levy (Sales Tax Handbook, 2019). The electorate in Iowa and Ohio may approve a school district income tax levy in addition to a property tax levy (Walczak, 2019). California schools may petition voters to approve a rise in parcel tax; however, they may not request a property tax increase. Parcel tax levies impose a flat dollar amount per property (Ballotpedia, 2019b). Table 2.3 shows the authority to pass excess millage by jurisdiction.

**Table 2.3. Excess Millage Authority[a]**

| Jurisdiction[b] | Voter Approval | Community Budget Approval | Budget Vote (Jurisdiction Member) | Jurisdiction[b] | Voter Approval | Community Budget Approval | Budget Vote (Jurisdiction Member) |
|---|---|---|---|---|---|---|---|
| Alabama | X | | | Nebraska | X | | |
| Alaska | | | X (Borough) | Nevada | X | | |
| Arizona | | | X (School Board) | New Hampshire | | X | |
| Arkansas | X | | | New Jersey | X | | |
| California | Parcel tax only | | | New Mexico | X | | |
| Colorado | X | | | New York | | X | |
| Connecticut | | X | | North Dakota | X | | |
| Delaware | X | | | Ohio | X | | |
| Florida | X | | | Oklahoma | X | | |
| Georgia | X | | | Oregon | X | | |
| Idaho | X | | | Pennsylvania | X | | |
| Illinois | X | | | Rhode Island | | X | |
| Indiana | X | | | South Carolina | X | | |
| Iowa | X | | | South Dakota | | | X (School Board) |
| Kansas | X | | | Tennessee | | | X (County or City Council) |
| Kentucky[c] | X | | | Texas | | | X (School Board) |
| Louisiana | X | | | Utah | X | | |
| Maine | | X | | Vermont | | X | |

| State | | | |
|---|---|---|---|
| Maryland | | X (County or City Council) | |
| Michigan | X | | |
| Minnesota | X | | |
| Mississippi | X | | |
| Missouri | X | | |
| Montana | X | | |
| Virginia[d] | | X | |
| Washington | | X | |
| Washington, DC | | | X (City Council) |
| West Virginia | | X | |
| Wisconsin | | X | |
| Wyoming | | X | |

Sources: Ballotpedia (2019) and Lincoln Institute of Land Policy (2018).
Notes: [a] The table does not list dependent school districts in Massachusetts and North Carolina because these districts do not have taxing authority. The parent government in these states proposes referendums for excess tax millage.
[b] The table does not list Hawaii because this jurisdiction does not authorize local property tax.
[c] When a school district wants to raise the tax rate more than 4 percent from the previous year, residents must vote on the matter.
[d] Virginia's dependent districts with a parent government do not have taxing authority; however, the lone independent school district has taxing authority.

## PROPERTY TAX RELIEF PROGRAMS

To reduce property tax for specific taxpayers and businesses, all 50 states and the District of Columbia implement programs to ease the burden (Lincoln Institute of Land Policy, 2018). Property tax abatement applies to a property tax reduction or immunity granted by a governmental agent (e.g., county) to businesses and specific individuals on rare occasions that propose community economic development. When considering tax abatements, school officials should negotiate with businesses and governmental entities to prevent district property tax losses, if permitted by law.

Although every state's tax abatement program differs, only Alabama, California, Kansas, Michigan, and Mississippi exclude school officials from abatement decisions. Colorado, Connecticut, Maine, Oklahoma, and Vermont reimburse school districts for financial losses due to abatements (Lincoln Institute of Land Policy, 2018).

Forty-one states protect certain homeowners (e.g., military veterans, widows, low-income property owners, or elderly) from excessive property tax charges with a circuit breaker or homestead exemption program. Each state plan differs by eligibility criteria and income levels (i.e., thresholds). Thirty-three states and the District of Columbia maintain a circuit breaker program (Lincoln Institute of Land Policy, 2018). A circuit breaker permits property tax relief for eligible taxpayers who earn below a certain income level. Tax reductions in circuit breakers generally exempt a specific dollar amount from the property tax bill (Brimley et al., 2020).

A homestead exemption functions similarly to a circuit breaker, and often these terms are interchangeable. However, to draw a distinction, a homestead exemption relieves a part of an eligible applicant's home value from taxation. Reductions may reduce a percentage of the fair market value or lower the assessed value on an owner-occupied property using a flat rate or fixed amount (Brimley et al., 2020).

Ohio's homestead exemption program, by example, benefits low-income senior citizens and permanently disabled persons. Eligible seniors obtain a $25,000 reduction on an owner-occupied home's fair market value. Ohio also grants an across-the-board, owner-occupied homestead exemption (i.e., rollback) for all property taxpayers at any income level. This 10 percent rollback decreases the property tax commitment on a principle residence (Lincoln Institute of Land Policy, 2018; Maxwell & Sweetland, 2013). Ohio and a few other states reimburse school districts to lessen the circuit breaker or homestead exemption revenue loss. The state legislature in these instances appropriates monies for the reimbursement.

To view residential property tax relief programs for a specific state, click or search for the Lincoln Institute of Land Policy website at https://www .lincolninst.edu/research-data/data-toolkits/significant-features-property-tax/ access-property-tax-database/property-tax-in-detail, select a state and year, and click residential property tax relief programs.

## PROPERTY TAX BILL

A property tax bill commonly shows a property owner (e.g., private party; commercial, industrial, or utility company; or farmer) a parcel's assessed value, effective millage rate, exemption, and tax obligation. The local tax collector or treasurer normally sends the tax bill to property owners twice a year. The owner's mortgage company pays the tax bill for the property owner without the taxpayer's knowledge when assigned.

Landholders pay property taxes in arrears, meaning the owner pays for the previous year's tax liability during the current year. When an initial excess property levy passes, the school district does not receive the yield for approximately 2 years after voter approval. The tax collector (e.g., county treasurer) collects the individual property tax and distributes the aggregate revenue to school districts and other taxing subdivisions. When a property owner does not pay the assessment by the deadline, the tax collector charges a delinquent late fee to the property owner (Redmond, 2018).

For clarification, an Ohioan's property tax bill can be explained in five steps:

1. The county auditor establishes the property's fair market value.
2. When a taxpayer is disabled or 65 years of age or older with an adjusted gross income less than $32,200, the fair market value decreases up to $25,000 for the owner-occupied homestead exemption to form the net assessed value.
3. The auditor now multiplies the net assessed value by Ohio's 35 percent assessment ratio for residential property.
4. The auditor then multiplies the net assessed value (i.e., taxable value) by the effective millage rate, which yields the prerollback tax obligation.
5. The auditor subsequently multiplies the prerollback tax obligation by 10 percent and subtracts this reduction to establish the final tax duty.

For example, when an Ohioan's owner-occupied home has a fair market value of $100,000 with a $25,000 deduction for a senior or disabled person's homestead exemption, the home's assessed value is $75,000. To compute the net assessed value, the auditor applies Ohio's 35 percent assessment ratio for residential property, which equals a net assessed value of $26,250. The net assessed value is then multiplied by an effective millage rate (.0375 or 37.5 mills) to compute the prerollback tax of $984.38. With Ohio's 10 percent rollback, the tax due is $885.94.

Figure 2.1 displays an actual California property tax bill. The assessed land and improvement values minus exemptions equal the net assessed value within designation A. Label B displays the various property tax subdivisions (e.g., city, water district, school district, and community college) amounts approved by the voters with millage rates. Marker C describes other directly assessed taxes, including the school district parcel tax. Indicator D shows the payment installments (Legislative Analyst's Office, 2012; Local Television for Santa Cruz, 2019).

The general tax list (i.e., tax roll) and tax duplicate catalogs all the properties with corresponding classifications within a district's boundaries. As stated by the Office of the Assessor (2019), the local tax authority (i.e., auditor, tax collector, and assessor)

- maintains the tax list and duplicate;
- identifies all individual properties within the district by classification;
- authorizes the fair market value by parcel;
- oversees the mass property appraisal and reappraisal process;
- calculates a property's assessed value by classification and appropriate assessment ratio;

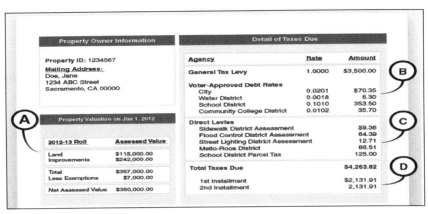

**Figure 2.1. California Tax Bill**

*Source:* Legislative Analyst's Office. (2012). *Understanding California's property taxes.* Sacramento, CA: Author.

- computes the district's aggregate property tax base by assessed classifications;
- bills property owners, collects property tax, and issues delinquency notices; and
- computes the district's property tax yield and distributes the proceeds to school districts.

Because tax authorities fulfill these tasks, school administrators and CFO/treasurers are fortunate, although periodic checks by school personnel remain fruitful.

## SALES SURTAX

A number of states permit local sales surtax for unrestricted public school income. The local sales surtax applies to most tangible goods, although many states exempt food, prescription drugs, and clothing (Sales Tax Handbook, 2019).

Sales tax is easy to collect because the seller or vendor collects the tax from the customer at the point of sale and remits cumulative collections on a monthly basis to a state agency (e.g., Department of Revenue or Taxation). The agency disburses the funds monthly to the eligible local government subdivision (e.g., independent school district or county). Sales tax, a proportional tax, imposes the same percentage rate on each purchase to all buyers regardless of a person's income level. Because local sales surtax collection is immediate as opposed to property tax, the district accepts sales surtax income soon after collection, even when voter approval is necessary (Brimley et al., 2020).

Parent governments with dependent school districts often collect local sales surtax and share the proceeds via an intergovernmental agreement. Dependent school districts in Alaska, Arizona, California, Louisiana, New York, Maryland, Massachusetts, Mississippi, New Jersey, New York, Rhode Island, Texas, Virginia, and Wisconsin share their parent government's local sales surtax (Sales Tax Handbook, 2019).

By law in Tennessee, counties allocate one-half of the local sales surtax collection to public school districts (County Technical Assistance Service, 2019). Counties in North Carolina, by statute, must reserve 30 percent of the local sales surtax proceeds to public schools for capital outlay; however, 10 districts allocated local sales surtax monies for operating expenses (Civitas Institute, 2018).

Independent school districts in Georgia, Nevada, and Louisiana may levy local sales surtax for unrestricted revenue (Sales Tax Handbook, 2019).

Independent school districts in five New York counties share a portion of local sales surtax. For example, schools in New York's Westchester County received 16.67 percent of the county's 1 percent local sales surtax (New York State Department of Education, 2019). For illustration, Bedford Central School District in Westchester County collected $1,600,000 from county sales surtax in the 2019 fiscal year (see appendix-exhibit 2).

Small schools with inhabitants of less than 125,000 in New York may impose up to 3 percent of a consumer's utility bill as a local excise (i.e., sales) tax (New York State Department of Education, 2019). To calculate the dollars a school district collects from local sales surtax is quite simple. The district's (i.e., aggregate) local utility sales tax base multiplied by the authorized percentage equals the yield. For example, New York's Watervliet City Schools (2018) with a district utility sales tax base of $10,833,333 and a 3 percent utility sales surtax rate yielded $325,000 in actual local utility sales surtax collection in the 2018 fiscal year with the same amount estimated for the 2019 fiscal year (see appendix-exhibit 3).

## INCOME SURTAX

Local income surtax is separate from federal, state, or municipal income tax. Kentucky, Ohio, Pennsylvania, and Iowa allow independent school districts to levy a local income surtax for school operations. Taxpayers pay local income surtax through payroll withholdings, quarterly estimated payments, or annual returns (Walczak 2019).

In Ohio, the state administers the school district income surtax collection after district voters approve an income tax–operating levy. The referendum states the request in a fractional percentage (i.e., .25 percent) and authorizes the collection from 1 to 5 years. Taxpayers immediately pay the local income surtax by payroll withholdings after an affirmative levy. Currently, 199 of Ohio's 612 school districts collect local income surtax (Walczak 2019).

Kentucky permits school districts to tax income through a county occupational license tax, which applies to workers' wages and businesses' net profits. The county collects and administers the tax. Based on the community, charges range from 0.5 percent to 2 percent of taxable income (Hall & Koumpias, 2016; Walczak 2019).

By ordinance or resolution, a Pennsylvania school district and municipality may impose up to 1 percent on an individual's taxable income (Local Government Commission, 2017). (Note: This source is published every 3 years; a new edition will be available in 2020.) Local tax collection agencies collect the earned income tax and split the proceeds evenly between the school district and municipality. In Pennsylvania, 472 school districts levy a local income surtax (Walczak 2019).

For those authorized schools in Ohio, Kentucky, and Pennsylvania, calculating an aggregate local income surtax yield is simple. The income surtax yield formula is the district's local income tax base multiplied by the authorized percentage rate, equaling the yield. By example, Ohio's Bexley City Schools' (2019) income tax base ($838,717,733) multiplied by the income surtax rate (.0075 percent) yielded the district $6,290,383 in local revenue (see appendix-exhibit 4).

Iowa permits a local income surtax assessed as a percentage of a person's taxable income. School districts may set income surtax rates up to 20 percent by voter approval; however, rates usually range between 6 and 10 percent. The state collects the tax on the district's behalf, when taxpayers file their state income tax. Eighty-two percent of all Iowa school districts collect this surtax (Iowa School Boards Association, 2018). To tabulate a taxpayer's income surtax obligation, an individual's duty equals an individual's collected tax multiplied by the surtax rate. The district's income surtax yield totals the residents' aggregate state tax collection multiplied by the surtax percentage rate.

Dependent school districts across the country with a parent government typically share a portion of the local income surtax, which is comingled with other unrestricted funds. For example, dependent school districts in Maryland and the District of Columbia share local income surtax with the county and city governments, respectively. In Maryland, school district income surtax revenue produced nearly 20 percent of a school's total local revenue. Due to Maryland's dependent school structure, the taxing authority rests with the county government (Department of Legislative Services, 2018).

Similar to local sales surtax, income surtax collection is immediate unlike property tax. When voters approve a local income surtax levy, the district receives the surtax revenue soon after collection. Income tax is a progressive tax because the more wages an individual earns, the more money is due normally. Tax analysts view income tax as a fairer duty than sales and property tax (Odden & Picus, 2020).

## SUPPLEMENTARY TAXES

A number of states grant independent school districts the authority to levy specific local supplementary taxes, with the aim of offsetting the reliance on property tax. Independent schools accept these funds from the treasuring agent at the local or state level. For dependent school districts, the parent government obtains the supplementary taxes via a local or state governmental agency and shares the revenue with the school districts. When state law permits, independent and dependent districts may authorize the following supplementary local taxes:

1. Amusement tax in three states (see table 2.6) specifies a proportional tax on admission prices to places of amusement, entertainment, and recreation. This tax is often shared by the county (Local Government Commission, 2017; Maryland Association of Counties, 2019; Walczak, Kaeding, & Drenkard, 2018).
2. Business privilege tax in Pennsylvania depicts a proportional tax levied on the gross receipts from certain trades, merchants, vendors, or professions for the privilege of doing business within the taxing district (Local Government Commission, 2017).
3. Excise tax in 11 states indicates a selective sales tax available to school districts levied on gross proceeds from sales on specific services or goods, such as vehicles, tobacco, and alcohol. A sales tax on tobacco, alcohol, or marijuana is commonly termed a sin tax. A sin tax or regressive tax appears to be unfair in distribution because this type of tax imposes a greater tax burden on low-income people who spend a greater proportion of earned income on such items than high-income people spend. Excise tax may also be charged on fuel, lodging, or motor vehicle sales and rentals (Brimley et al., 2020).
4. Franchise tax in three states denotes a duty on a business's net worth, net income, or profits (Walczak et al., 2018).
5. Local services tax in Pennsylvania assesses a tax on an individual's occupation (Local Government Commission, 2017; Walczak et al., 2018).
6. Occupational license tax in three states signifies a proportional tax assessed on the occupation of persons who reside within the taxing district (Local Government Commission, 2017; Walczak et al., 2018).
7. Parcel tax in California designates a flat rate tax that considers a property's square footage and age; this tax does not distinguish assessed value (Ballotpedia, 2019b).
8. Per capita tax in two states charges a flat percentage on an adult's residency within a tax jurisdiction, regardless of employment or income. Dependent districts in Maryland collect a share of this tax through the parent government (i.e., county), and school districts in Pennsylvania may collect this funding (Maryland Association of Counties, 2019; Walczak et al., 2018).
9. Real estate transfer tax in seven states authorizes a proportional tax, when an individual sells real estate. School districts in three states (see

table 2.6) receive a share of these funds. For example, municipalities and school districts in Pennsylvania equally split a local real estate transfer tax to a maximum 1 percent of the mortgage. Oklahoma county treasurers distribute the real estate transfer tax revenue to the county's Common School Fund. Hawaii solely dedicates this tax to school systems on a statewide basis, and Connecticut allows a local decision for schools to collect a real estate transfer tax (Lincoln Institute of Land Policy, 2018; Local Government Commission, 2017).

10. Severance tax in 18 states, the most popular local supplementary school tax, imposes a duty on the production or extraction of natural resources. This volatile tax is unstable due to collection variations from year to year. Nevada school districts receive a portion of severance tax proceeds in the same proportion as the shared property tax (Nevada Const., 2013).

11. Utility tax in eight states levies a tax on public utilities as a consumer use tax or a percentage of the utility company's gross sales (Maryland Association of Counties, 2019; New York State Department of Education, 2019). In Kentucky, schools receive a 3 percent consumer utility use tax on telephone, water, sewer, gas, electric, and cable services (Sherman, 2019).

12. Eleven states assess a motor vehicle property tax. Municipalities and boroughs in Alaska may assess motor vehicle property tax, exempt motor vehicles from property tax, or impose a registration fee in lieu of an ad valorem property tax (Lincoln Institute of Land Policy, 2018).

Table 2.4 presents the approved supplementary local tax sources by state. The corresponding numbers above refer to the designated tax. An S in the table means that districts share the local supplementary revenue, and an L refers to a locally established income source.

As table 2.4 indicates, Pennsylvania's tax codes allow the most supplementary local taxes for school districts. The Local Tax Enabling Act (53 Pa. C. S., 1965) sanctioned schools to choose from supplementary tax options, with the intention to reduce taxpayers' property tax burden. These taxes, often called nuisance taxes, characterize taxes that are an annoyance to collect, a bother to pay, and an insignificant portion of the school budget.

In an attempt to scale back nuisance taxes, Pennsylvania legislators passed the Omnibus Amendment (53 Pa. C. S., 1998), which approved school districts to levy a higher earned income or franchise tax in lieu of these nuisance taxes. Because this law simply encouraged choice, only a few schools executed changes (Local Government Commission, 2017; Walczak et al., 2018). Pennsylvania's Neshaminy School District (2018) estimated

**Table 2.4. Supplementary Local Tax[a]**

| State[b] | 1 | 2 | 3 | 4 | 5 | 6 | 7 | 8 | 9 | 10 | 11 | 12 |
|---|---|---|---|---|---|---|---|---|---|---|---|---|
| Alabama | X | | X | | | X | | | | X | X | X |
| Alaska | | | X-S | | | | | | | X-S | | X-S[c] |
| Arkansas | | | | | | | | | | X | | X |
| California | | | | | | | X | | | X | | |
| Colorado | | | | | | | | | | X | | |
| Connecticut | | | | | | | | | X-L | | | X |
| Florida | | | | | | | | | | | X | |
| Georgia | | | | | | | | | X-S | | | |
| Hawaii | | | | | | | | | X | | | |
| Idaho | | | X | | | X | | | | X | | |
| Indiana | | | X | | | | | | | | | |
| Iowa | | | | | | | | | | | X | |
| Kansas | | | | | | | | | | | | X |
| Kentucky | | | X | | | X | | | | X | X-S | |
| Maine | | | | | | | | | | | | |
| Maryland | X-S | | X-S | | | | | X-S | X-S | | X-S | |
| Massachusetts | | | X | | | | | | | | | |
| Minnesota | | | | | | | | | | X | | |
| Mississippi | | | | | | | | | | | X | X |
| Missouri | | | X | | | | | | | | | X |
| Montana | | | | | | | | | | X | | |
| Nebraska | | | | | | | | | | | X-S | |
| Nevada | | | | X | | | | | | X | | |
| New Hampshire | | | X | | | | | | | | | |
| New Mexico | | | X | | | | | | | X | | |
| New York | | | | | | | | | | | X-S | |
| North Carolina | | | | | | | | | X-S | | | X-S |
| North Dakota | | | | | | | | | | X | | |
| Oklahoma | | | | | | | | | X | X-S | | |
| Ohio | | | | | | | | | | X | | |
| Pennsylvania | X | X | | X | X | X | | X | | X-L | | |
| South Carolina | | | | | | | | | | | | X |

| State[b] | 1 | 2 | 3 | 4 | 5 | 6 | 7 | 8 | 9 | 10 | 11 | 12 |
|---|---|---|---|---|---|---|---|---|---|---|---|---|
| South Dakota | | | | X | | | | | | X | | |
| Tennessee | | | X-S | | | | | | | X-S | | |
| Virginia | | | | | | | | | | | | X-S |
| Washington | | | | | | | | | | X | | |
| West Virginia | | | | | | | | | | | | X |
| Wyoming | | | | | | | | | X-S | | | |
| States | 3 | 1 | 11 | 3 | 1 | 3 | 1 | 2 | 7 | 18 | 8 | 11 |

*Sources:* Ballotpedia (2019b), Lincoln Institute of Land Policy (2018), Maryland Association of Counties (2019); Sales Tax Handbook (2019), and Walczak, Kaeding, & Drenkard (2018).
*Notes:* [a]Data for this table were cross-referenced from many sources. Because of the multitude of sources necessary for this table, a number of sources were omitted.
[b]The table does not list Arizona, Delaware, Illinois, Louisiana, Michigan, New Jersey, Oregon, Rhode Island, Texas, Vermont, Wisconsin, and the District of Columbia because the school districts in these governing bodies do not collect supplementary local tax.
[c]Alaskan municipalities and boroughs may assess motor vehicle property tax, exempt motor vehicles from property tax, or impose a registration fee in lieu of an ad valorem tax.

revenue at $5,968,149 from Act 511 supplementary local tax sources in the 2019 fiscal year, which denoted 3.3 percent of the total district revenue (see appendix-exhibit 1).

## NONTAX REVENUE

A school district's nontax local revenue may include tuition, transportation fees, textbook sales and rentals, school lunch purchases, district activity receipts, service income, royalties, facility rentals, property transactions, investment earnings, fines, private contributions, and student fees (U.S. Census Bureau, 2019b). Athletic gate receipts, typically, only pay for athletic expenditures instead of general fund costs. South Dakota public school districts accept local revenue from traffic fines issued within the county, when infractions occur (Sioux Falls School District, 2019).

## FUNDING FOR NONPUBLIC AND PUBLIC CHARTER SCHOOLS

### Nonpublic Schools

Nonpublic schools, including religious institutions, by law, may not collect local tax for expenses; therefore, student tuition accounted for 70 to 80 percent of nonpublic schools' budgets. Grants, fund raising, endowments, private donations, parent association activities, and corporate giving complete the remaining ordinary local revenue sources for nonpublic schools (Daughtery, Hester, & Weatherill, 2016).

Nonpublic school students and parents do not generally benefit from local public monies for schools, but parents still pay local taxes (e.g., local sales tax, property, and income) and property tax, when they own a house or business. To lower the total taxes a person owes, individual tax credits and deductions allow families to receive state income tax relief for approved educational expenses, which can include private school tuition, books, supplies, computers, tutors, and transportation. Eight states (Alabama, Illinois, Indiana, Iowa, Louisiana, Minnesota, South Carolina, and Wisconsin) offer nonpublic school parents an individual income tax credit for a partial reimbursement of paid taxes (EdChoice, 2019).

Educational savings accounts (ESAs) allow parents to withdraw their children from public or charter schools and receive a deposit of public funds into government authorized savings accounts with varying uses. ESAs—often distributed to families via a debit card—can cover private school tuition and fees, online learning programs, private tutoring, and other approved learning services and materials. These plans are sponsored by states, state agencies, or educational institutions and authorized by Section 529 of the Internal Revenue Code. Arizona, Florida, Mississippi, Nevada, North Carolina, and Tennessee offer educational savings accounts (EdChoice, 2019).

Entrepreneurial events and nontax income sources could expand a nonpublic school's local revenue. Regardless of a family or child's religious affiliation, offerings may include summer camps (e.g., arts and adventure), tutorial and daycare centers, online curriculum, adult education programs, teacher institutes, auctions, or international school partnerships (Daughtery et al., 2016).

Student performances (e.g., ticket sales for plays) and off-season sporting events may increase local school revenue regardless of a family or child's religious affiliation. Tournament registrations for two-person beach volleyball, three-on-three basketball, or football passing leagues along with other activities may add potential opportunities to raise local money. Facility rentals and real estate holdings depict additional income means. Nonpublic school leaders, therefore, must "think outside the box" to earn extra local income for their schools.

## Public Charter Schools

Charter schools embody semiautonomous public schools that obtain public funding. Operating by a written contract with a state, district, or other entity (i.e., authorizer or sponsor), the contract (charter) details the school's organization and success indicators (e.g., student academic performance). Public charter schools do not charge student tuition.

Six states (Montana, Nebraska, North Dakota, South Dakota, Vermont, and West Virginia) do not have charter schools (Ziebarth, 2019). All other states base local charter funding on pupil enrollment, although per-pupil revenue dramatically varies within and across states. When a student enrolls in a charter school, local and state funds often follow the student from the resident school district to the charter school (Education Commission of the States, 2018b).

Education Commission of the States (2018b) reported that states devised three different charter school funding mechanisms. The charter student's resident school district, statewide formula, or charter school authorizer (e.g., state education agency, municipality, local school district, higher education institution, or not-for-profit organization) direct funding.

Alabama, Hawaii, Maryland, Massachusetts, New York, Ohio, Pennsylvania, and Rhode Island mandate districts grant a portion of local funds from the student's resident district. Charter schools in Arizona, Idaho, Maine, Minnesota, Missouri, and the District of Columbia acquire a flat per-pupil amount of local funds through the statewide formula. Thirty-one states base local charter school funding on the authorizing district's revenue. When the authorizer is not a local district, charter schools typically obtain the same local per-pupil monies as a school district in the charter school's location (Education Commission of the States, 2018b).

To see sanctioned charter school authorizers by state (Education Commission of the States, 2018c), click or search for the Education Commission of the States website at http://ecs.force.com/mbdata/mbquestNB2C?rep=CS1708. To view local funding allowances for charter schools by state, click or search for the Education Commission of the States website at http://ecs.force.com/mbdata/mbquestNB2C?rep=CS1716.

## SUMMARY

Across the United States, local school funding originates from a number of sources—tax on property, sales, and income; supplementary taxes; and nontax proceeds. Property tax remains the most productive local revenue. Fortunately for school officials, tax authorities (e.g., local collection agents and state revenue departments) collect revenue, compute calculations, and distribute monies to school districts; however, understanding the nature of each source and calculation derivatives are essential for school administrators and CFO/treasurers.

In this vein, school officials must grasp the distinctions of local school funding, particularly property tax methods and other potential local income sources. Nonpublic and public charter school administrators should thoroughly comprehend available local school funding opportunities in their state, precise funding means, and authorized methods to collect and increase local revenue.

## PROJECTS

1. Describe the governing structure of your school district.
2. Investigate and report a thorough search of property tax for your jurisdiction—classifications, corresponding assessment ratios, assessment administration (i.e., reappraisal cycles), exemptions, tangible personal property, as well as residential tax relief and incentive programs. Click or search for the Lincoln Institute of Land Policy website at https://www.lincolninst .edu/research-data/data-toolkits/significant-features-property-tax/access -property-tax-database/property-tax-in-detail, select a state, and retrieve this data.
3. Create a list of all the potential local funding sources for your school district, including tax and nontax revenues.
4. Examine and report your property tax bill or an example of one from your locale. Classify and report the following on the property:
   a. classification,
   b. fair market value,
   c. assessment ratio,
   d. assessed value,
   e. property tax relief, when obtainable,
   f. governmental taxing subdivisions,
   g. effective millage rate(s), and
   h. tax obligation.
5. Examine your school or another school's budget. Chart and record the following for the fiscal year:
   a. school district valuation,
   b. property tax base,
   c. effective millage rate(s),
   d. property tax yield,
   e. other local tax yields (e.g., local sales, income, and supplementary tax),
   f. nontax revenue (e.g., tuition and building rentals, etc.), and
   g. total local revenue.

6. Discover and recount the approaches your school may pursue to collect additional local operating funds.
7. Investigate the local school tax elections in your jurisdiction that authorize districts to impose taxes to fund the operation. Click or search for the Ballotpedia website at https://ballotpedia.org/Local_school_tax_on_the_ballot to retrieve this data.
8. Identify and record the available local funding for a nonpublic or charter school.

# Chapter Three

# State Revenue

## OBJECTIVES

After reading this chapter, you should be able to

✓ describe the state budget process (NELP 5.3, 6.1, 6.2, 6.3);
✓ differentiate between the various funding distribution methods and explain the specific model for your jurisdiction (NELP 5.3, 6.1, 6.2, 6.3); and
✓ understand categorical funds as well as entitlement and discretionary grants from your state (NELP 5.3, 6.1, 6.2, 6.3).

The Articles of Confederation (Art. of Conf.) governed the United States between 1781 and 1789. The Articles sanctioned each state as sovereign, free, and independent, thereby, limiting federal powers. The states' ratification of the U.S. Constitution (U.S. Const.) in 1789 strengthened federal powers; however, the Tenth Amendment (U.S. Const. amend. X) granted each state the power to create and administer laws not specifically stated in the Constitution (Alexander & Alexander, 2019). Laws and regulations, therefore, vary from state to state, although many functions regulated by states are universal, such as the following, according to Bowman and Kearney (2017):

• establishing elementary and secondary public education funding;
• forming and providing state schools, colleges, and universities;
• licensing and regulating businesses and professions;
• supporting state lands and parks;

- delivering public safety via state divisions for law enforcement, health, emergency management, environment, and fire science;
- administering state hospitals, housing, and nutrition programs;
- creating and sustaining state retirement systems, unemployment insurance, and workers' compensation;
- building and maintaining state highways and other conveyances; and
- establishing, collecting, and redistributing taxes.

States rely on a broad range of income sources to fund these functions. Most tax collections by a state fluctuate in response to state and national economic trends. When the economy booms, revenue rises; however, revenue falters in downturns. The total for states' unrestricted general fund revenue was almost $2 trillion in fiscal year 2017 (U.S. Census Bureau, 2019a).

State individual income tax generated 37.2 percent of the entire unrestricted tax revenue across the United States in the 2017 fiscal year, which is the most current data at the time of publication (U.S. Census Bureau, 2019a). Forty-one states and the District of Columbia levied broad-based individual income tax. New Hampshire and Tennessee taxed dividends and interest only as income, although Tennessee will phase out this tax beginning in 2021. Alaska, Florida, Nevada, South Dakota, Texas, Washington, and Wyoming did not have an individual state income tax (Loughead & Wei, 2019).

General sales tax, another unrestricted general fund income, produced 31.8 percent of the states' aggregate taxes in 2017. The remaining taxes in 2017 originated from selective excise sales, 16 percent; licenses, 5.8 percent; corporate net income, 4.7 percent; and other taxes, 4.5 percent (U.S. Census Bureau, 2019a). Forty-five states and the District of Columbia collected statewide sales tax. Alaska, Delaware, Montana, New Hampshire, and Oregon did not assess a statewide sales tax (Cammanga, 2019).

States assessed excise sales tax on alcoholic beverages, amusements, motor fuels, public utilities, and/or tobacco products. States may account for these funds in the unrestricted general fund or restricted accounts (U.S. Census Bureau, 2019a).

Property tax exemplifies a significant local government revenue, but this tax remains insignificant as a state tax source. The income from state-levied property tax represented less than 1 percent of the entire state revenue in 29 states (U.S. Census Bureau, 2019a).

State-levied property tax in Arkansas, Michigan, Montana, New Hampshire, Washington, and Wyoming denoted around 5 percent of each state's overall proceeds. Vermont counted heavily on this income source, which represented 26 percent of the state's entire receipts. Colorado, Connecticut, Delaware, Hawaii, Idaho, Iowa, New York, North Carolina, Ohio, Oklahoma,

South Dakota, Tennessee, Texas, and Utah did not collect a state-levied property tax (U.S. Census Bureau, 2019a).

Excluding taxes, state revenue also derived from nontax means (U.S. Census Bureau, 2019a), including

- federal public assistance grants through intergovernmental transfers, such as Medicaid;
- trust fund contributions to accounts for state pension, unemployment insurance, and workers' compensation;
- user charges, highway and transit tolls, higher education tuition, and state hospital payments;
- earnings on state-owned water, gas, and electric utility companies along with liquor stores;
- sales from state property transactions;
- investment returns from interest and dividends; and
- income from registration fees, licenses, permits, fines, penalties, and gambling proceeds.

A state's general fund does not include restricted income, earmarked for specific purposes. States collected restricted income from highway tolls, motor vehicle registration fees, and motor fuel tax to maintain transportation systems, with proceeds deposited into a specific account (U.S. Census Bureau, 2019a). To the contrary, a number of states designated legalized gambling monies to the general fund or a dedicated account targeted for particular programs, such as education, tourism, or environmental beautification. All states, except Hawaii and Utah, collected revenue from lottery operations, casinos, horse racetrack-casinos, or pari-mutuel wagering (U.S. Census Bureau, 2019a).

Governors and state legislatures consider competing demands to discern public spending priorities, while balancing the budget as mandated by each state's law. Aggregate expenditures in 2017 for all states were $2.3 trillion, including restricted intergovernmental transfers (e.g., shared Medicaid taxes between the state and federal government), which represented 23.8 percent of total spending. The 2017 general fund expenditures ($2 trillion) by service function with percentages of total spending included primary, secondary, and higher public education, 34.6 percent; welfare, 34 percent; health and hospitals, 7.6 percent; transportation, 6.5 percent; police protection and corrections, 3.5 percent; natural resources and parks, 1.5 percent; and all other general fund spending, 12.3 percent (U.S. Census Bureau, 2019a).

The National Association of State Budget Officers (2019) indicated that most states' budgets were currently in the black with a positive balance. States, however, tend to spend cautiously or stockpile reserve funds during predictions of slow economic growth. Norcross and Gonzalez (2018) reported that Alaska, South Dakota, Wyoming, North Dakota, and Florida were among the nation's most solvent states with high cash balances and assets. Illinois, Connecticut, Massachusetts, Pennsylvania, and California, by contrast, ranked at the bottom of all states with low cash reserves, expenses that exceeded revenue, high debt, and massive unfunded pension obligations.

## BUDGET PROCESS

State politicians govern policy priorities and allocate fiscal resources among competing pressures through a budgetary process. States administer both an operating and capital budget. The operating budget establishes funding for the operation of state agencies and programs, including primary and secondary public education. The capital budget authorizes appropriations associated with land acquisition or the construction of state buildings, including schoolhouses. This section solely examines state operating budgets.

As per the National Association of State Budget Officers (2019), 30 states and the District of Columbia created their operating budget on an annual cycle, meaning that the budget designated funding for 1 year. The other 20 states implemented a biennial budget adopted for a two-year fiscal period. Table 3.1 represents the operating budget cycle applied by each jurisdiction reported by the National Association of State Budget Officers (2015) in the most current *Budget Processes in the States*, which is a significant reference for state budget officers and others interested in the operation of state governments. According to a National Association of State Budget Officers official, the organization publishes an updated report every 5 years with a new edition scheduled for 2020 (K. Versey-White, personal communication, August 27, 2019).

Although budget cycles vary from state to state (see table 3.1), the National Association of State Budget Officers (2015) listed the following common actions:

- The state office of budget and management staff provides guidance to state agencies (e.g., department of education), accepts each division's funding requests, and then consolidates all submissions into a statewide budget proposal.
- After a review and analysis of the agencies' budget requests, the state office of budget and management staff creates a budget recommendation for the governor, which becomes the proposal to the state legislature.
- Legislative committees, by chamber, review the governor's budget request, debate alternatives, and then approve their chamber version.
- A joint conference committee with legislators from both chambers join the two versions into one recommendation.

**Table 3.1. Budget Cycle**

| Jurisdiction | Budget Cycle | | Jurisdiction | Budget Cycle | |
|---|---|---|---|---|---|
| | Annual | Biennial | | Annual | Biennial |
| Alabama | X | | Nebraska | | X |
| Alaska | X | | Nevada | | X |
| Arizona | X | | New Hampshire | | X |
| Arkansas | | X | New Jersey | X | |
| California | X | | New Mexico | X | |
| Colorado | X | | New York | X | |
| Connecticut | | X | North Carolina | | X |
| Delaware | X | | North Dakota | | X |
| Florida | X | | Ohio | | X |
| Georgia | X | | Oklahoma | X | |
| Hawaii | | X | Oregon | | X |
| Idaho | X | | Pennsylvania | X | |
| Illinois | X | | Rhode Island | X | |
| Indiana | | X | South Carolina | X | |
| Iowa | X | | South Dakota | X | |
| Kansas | X | | Tennessee | X | |
| Kentucky | | X | Texas | | X |
| Louisiana | X | | Utah | X | |
| Maine | | X | Vermont | X | |
| Maryland | X | | Virginia | | X |
| Massachusetts | X | | Washington | | X |
| Michigan | X | | Washington, DC | X | |
| Minnesota | | X | West Virginia | X | |
| Mississippi | X | | Wisconsin | | X |
| Missouri | X | | Wyoming | | X |
| Montana | | X | Total | 31 | 20 |

*Source:* National Association of State Budget Officers (2015).
*Note:* Data from the *Budget Processes in the States*, which is a significant reference for state budget officers and others interested in the operation of state governments, are current at the time of publication. The National Association of State Budget Officers (NASBO) publishes an updated report every 5 years with a new edition scheduled for 2020 according to a NASBO official.

- After each chamber passes the consolidated budget resolution, the governor may sign the bill into law.

Because the business or fiscal year begins on July 1 in most states, a budget bill enactment and appropriation must occur prior to that date for spending purposes. The fiscal year in Michigan, Alabama, and the District of Columbia opens on October 1. Texas commences the fiscal year on September 1; New York begins on April 1 (National Association of State Budget Officers, 2015).

Throughout the entire funding cycle, the state office of budget and management staff directs the accounting, auditing, and managing of the state's finances. To view the operating budgetary cycle timeframe for a state or the District of Columbia, click or search for table 1: Budget Calendar in the *Budget Processes in the States* at https://www.nasbo.org/reports-data/budget -processes-in-the-states.

States employ different approaches to develop their budget. Incremental; line-item; performance-based; zero-based; and the budgeting planning, programming, budgeting, and evaluation (PPBE) system were the recognized methods (National Association of State Budget Officers, 2015).

Legislators employ the planning, programming, budgeting, and evaluation system approach by first defining goals and analyzing strategies within the planning and programming phases. During the budgeting stage, state budget offices establish, justify, and execute total revenues and expenditures. State budget and management office staffs modify budgets during the evaluation phase. When substantiated, unmet goals in a fiscal year extend to the next year based on governor and legislative initiatives. Changes in long-range plans, a lack of consensus, and limited cost data restrict the PPBE method (National Association of State Budget Officers, 2015).

Incremental budgeting assigns a set percentage increase or decrease from the previous year's funding level to resolve the next year's budget allocation. An incremental budget is simple because the state budget and management office staff establishes percentage increases or decreases by allocations. The instituted percentages then apply to the previous budget's dollars to shape the next financial plan allotment. When overall budget needs are greater than the supplied percentage increase in an incremental budget, adjustments become necessary; otherwise, demands remain unmet (Brimley et al., 2020).

Line-item budgeting considers each budget line (e.g., fund, function, and object) and examines historical expenditures and revenue data. The line-item budget development process is basic and straightforward in preparation, although decision makers may find that this approach presents meager financial data on specific performance in budgeted areas (Brimley et al., 2020).

Performance-based budgeting, also known as results-based or outcome-based costing, links allocations to outcomes and accordingly assigns funds. Brimley et al. (2020) maintained this mechanism necessitates a thoughtful, deliberate approach to link funding with program effectiveness and efficiency. This process consumes time due to considerations for input and output indicators to evaluate cost-effective variables.

Zero-based budgeting compels the budgeting process to start from zero without any reference to previous funding levels. Brimley et al. (2020) asserted this strategy necessitated an evaluation of all programs within the budget, which was a rather complicated process.

The National Association of State Budget Officers (2015) reported each jurisdiction's budgetary process and indicated that 30 states recognized incremental budgeting as their primary approach. Thirteen states utilized the planning, programming, budgeting, and evaluation system. Three states developed their budgets with a line-item approach, and three other states and the District of Columbia employed a performance-based budgeting process as the primary approach in conjunction with incremental budgeting. Oregon was the only state to distinguish zero-based budgeting as the primary budget approach, and 12 states listed this approach as complementary.

To examine the primary budget development strategy for a state, click or search for table 12: Budget Approach in the *Budget Processes in the States* at https://www.nasbo.org/reports-data/budget-processes-in-the-states.

When legislators debate the budget bill's allocations, questions arise regarding how much money to allot state agencies, including primary and secondary public education. Due to periodic court orders to address legal challenges for equitable and adequate public education monies, Odden and Picus (2020) affirmed that consultants occasionally work with state legislatures to assess public education delivery systems and funding levels. As per Odden and Picus (2020), states may employ one of four cost study methodologies to confirm funding amounts:

- The successful school/district method scrutinizes districts with prominent student performances, analyzes the average expenditures in those districts to achieve success, assumes similar outcomes with comparable funding for other districts, and accordingly proposes funds.
- The professional judgment strategy utilizes a panel of educators who distinguish resources (e.g., number of teachers, kind of materials, quality of facilities, and programs) that a prototypical school needs to garner successful academic student performances and recommends that specific funding level.

- The evidence-based design considers research to classify comprehensive school operations that produce effective student academic performances, calculates how much those specifics cost to implement, and then recommends the monies to support such factors.
- The cost function approach employs statistical models to analyze relationships between effectual student educational performances associated with district spending and sets funding levels based upon findings.

Other state budget information, such as the governor's budget authority, responsibility, and veto powers, may be found in the *Budget Processes in the States* (National Association of State Budget Officers, 2015). Generally, legislators attempt to equalize funding to districts based on districts' fiscal capacity and ability to pay for educational opportunities (Odden & Picus, 2020).

## FUNDING DESCRIPTIONS BY JURISDICTION

Each state legislature and the city council in the District of Columbia establish a system for distributing school districts' unrestricted basic aid, often referenced as equalization aid. Each jurisdiction's (i.e., states and the District of Columbia) funding formula is a compilation of laws passed over the years, and the formula evolves with mounting levels of complexity. With serial attempts to improve the funding outcome, legislators, on occasion, attempt to dispatch lawsuits, categorize special needs for students and districts, and address accessible financial sources. As such, each legislative budgetary session may generate amendments to modify the existing formula (Brimley et al., 2020).

Each jurisdiction's formula employs a method to count students and incorporates other distinctive variables to calculate a school district's basic aid (Odden & Picus, 2020). Table 3.2 lists each jurisdiction's type of funding distribution model.

## BASIC AID FUNDING DISTRIBUTION MODELS

During the 1900s, states distributed monies to school districts with a flat grant formula that fixed a set per-student dollar amount regardless of a district's fiscal capacity. North Carolina is the only state that institutes a modified flat grant to distribute state basic aid. In the 1920s, foundation models became popular in allocating state basic aid, with the addition of a factor in the formula to address a district's fiscal capacity to raise local property tax (Brimley

**Table 3.2.  Basic Aid Distribution Model**

| Jurisdiction | Distribution Model | Jurisdiction | Distribution Model |
|---|---|---|---|
| Alabama | Modified Foundation | Nebraska | Modified Foundation |
| Alaska | Modified Foundation | Nevada | Modified Foundation |
| Arizona | Modified Power Equalization | New Hampshire | Modified Foundation |
| Arkansas | Modified Foundation | New Jersey | Modified Foundation |
| California | Hybrid | New Mexico | Modified Foundation |
| Colorado | Modified Foundation | New York | Hybrid |
| Connecticut | Hybrid | North Carolina | Modified Flat Grant |
| Delaware | Modified Power Equalization | North Dakota | Modified Foundation |
| Florida | Modified Power Equalization | Ohio | Modified Foundation |
| Georgia | Hybrid | Oklahoma | Hybrid |
| Hawaii | Modified Full Funding | Oregon | Modified Foundation |
| Idaho | Modified Foundation | Pennsylvania | Modified Foundation |
| Illinois | Modified Power Equalization | Rhode Island | Modified Foundation |
| Indiana | Modified Foundation | South Carolina | Modified Foundation |
| Iowa | Modified Foundation | South Dakota | Modified Foundation |
| Kansas | Modified Foundation | Tennessee | Modified Foundation |
| Kentucky | Hybrid | Texas | Hybrid |
| Louisiana | Modified Foundation | Utah | Hybrid |
| Maine | Modified Foundation | Vermont | Modified Power Equalization |
| Maryland | Modified Foundation | Virginia | Modified Foundation |
| Massachusetts | Modified Foundation | Washington | Modified Foundation |
| Michigan | Modified Power Equalization | Washington, DC | Modified Foundation |
| Minnesota | Modified Foundation | West Virginia | Modified Foundation |
| Mississippi | Modified Foundation | Wisconsin | Modified Power Equalization |
| Missouri | Modified Foundation | Wyoming | Modified Foundation |
| Montana | Hybrid | | |

*Source:* Verstegen (2018).

et al., 2020). Thirty-two states and the District of Columbia execute a modified foundation model (Verstegen, 2018).

The full funding model, similar to a flat grant, emerged in 1930, with the state accepting full responsibility for all school revenue. During the 1930s, states modified full funding formulas to address the costs associated with educating special populations, such as at-risk students (Brimley et al., 2020). Hawaii exercises the full funding model (Verstegen, 2018).

The power equalization model, popularized by *Serrano v. Priest* (1971), apportioned monies to equalize funding in correlation with a district's assessed property valuation. Seven states employ a modified power equalization model. Nine states utilize a hybrid of models to allocate state funds with concepts from two or more models (Verstegen, 2018).

## Flat Grant Model

The flat grant model distributes unrestricted state aid based on an equal perpupil subsidy established by the state legislature (Odden & Picus, 2020). In a conventional format, the formula divides the number of primary and secondary public school students in the state by the legislative appropriation. Using the conventional flat grant formula in the 2019 fiscal year, North Carolina charter school funding, with a statewide allocation of $674,314,240 and an average daily attendance (ADA) of 111,604 charter students in the state, awarded $6,042 per student (Public School Forum, 2019). North Carolina charter schools also accepted additional per-pupil formula funds for each attending child with special needs and limited English proficiency (Public School Forum, 2019).

To fund traditional public school districts, North Carolina employs a modified flat grant formula (Brimley et al., 2020). The North Carolina Department of Public Instruction (2018) confirmed that the state distributed money based on a district's average daily membership. The sum of attendance days for district students during a month divided by the number of days in the month equals the district's average daily membership. The state formula then applies the designated average daily membership throughout the legislative allocations in three allotments: position, dollar, and categorical (North Carolina Department of Public Instruction, 2018):

- For the position allotment, the district receives a specific amount by certified role. Based on the district's average daily membership by grade-level ratios, the state department of public instruction designates staff members to assign the legislatively approved salary and benefits for classroom teachers, building administrators, regular instructional support staff, and vocational personnel. The prescribed formula multiplies the legislatively approved positions by the state average salary per certification. The legislature, through the budgetary process, prescribes benefit amounts for health insurance, retirement, and social security.
- Dollar allotments set by the legislature include amounts for specific purposes, such as central office administration, teacher assistants, noninstructional staff, materials, supplies, and equipment.
- Categorical allocations subsidize specific services for disabled, disadvantaged, gifted/talented, at-risk, and limited English language students plus transporta-

tion services (e.g., bus drivers' salaries and benefits, fuel, maintenance, and bus replacements). This prescription establishes a district's categorical aid.

Supplemental allocations within the formula reflect a district's geographic and economic conditions (i.e., small county and property-poor school). Allotments comprise funding for driver's training and textbooks (North Carolina Department of Public Instruction, 2018). Figure 3.1 illustrates the proposed state aid for Alleghany County Schools during the 2019 fiscal year with an average daily membership of 1,362 students.

| North Carolina Public School Allotment | Alleghany County Schools |
|---|---|
| Position: Classroom Teachers (63.5 approved positions (salaries + benefits) | $4,115,694 |
| Position: School Building Administration (salaries + benefits) | $490,680 |
| Position: Central Office Administration (salaries + benefits) | $496,346 |
| Position: Instructional Support (6 approved positions (salaries + benefits) | $471,102 |
| Position: Career and Technical Education Teachers (salaries + benefits) | $770,412 |
| Dollar: Central Office Academically and Intellectually Gifted Students | $73,406 |
| Dollar: Teacher Assistants | $330,247 |
| Dollar: Non-instructional Support Personnel | $344,630 |
| Dollar: Instructional Supplies, Equipment, and Materials | $43,066 |
| Dollar: Career and Technical Education Program Support | $29,131 |
| Categorical/Dollar: Special Needs Students | $877,171 |
| Categorical/Dollar: Disadvantaged Students | $53,678 |
| Categorical/Dollar: Limited English Proficiency Students | $89,283 |
| Categorical/Dollar: At-Risk Student Services | $345,297 |
| Categorical/Dollar: Transportation | $423,293 |
| District Characteristic/Dollar – Small County Supplement | $1,548,700 |
| District Characteristic/Dollar – Low Wealth Supplement | -$0- |
| Other State Funding – Driver's Training | $30,123 |
| Other State Funding – Textbooks | $58,217 |
| | |
| **State Basic Aid** | $10,590,476 |

Figure 3.1.   Alleghany County Schools, Estimated FY 2019-State Basic

*Source:* North Carolina Department of Public Instruction. (2019b, September 9). State allotments. Retrieved from http://www.ncpublicschools.org/fbs/allotments/state/.

The conventional flat funding model appeals to policy leaders because this formula is easy to understand and simple to calculate, although most states have not applied this model for years. The equal subsidy set by educational components, such as the number of classroom teachers in relationship with the student headcount, appears to treat all districts fairly by allocating equal dollars for each student (Odden & Picus, 2020).

## Full Funding Model

In a full funding model, the state accepts complete responsibility for school funding. The full funding model appears similar to the flat funding model, although in this model the state assumes full responsibility for public education funding and does not permit schools to assess local monies. Similar to the flat grant model, schools acquire equally distributed monies in the full funding system; however, local revenue may not supplement state funding (Odden & Picus, 2020).

The classic full funding model also does not equalize factors related to a district's fiscal capacity nor local effort. When the legislature decides the total state apportionment, the allocation rarely covers district costs and often falls short in ensuring an adequate quality of education (Odden & Picus, 2020). Figure 3.2 shows a classic full funding formula.

**Figure 3.2.   Classic Full Funding Formula**
*Source:* Author created.

Hawaii is the only state in the Union that funds public schools with this arrangement. Hawaii's legislature resolves the primary and secondary public education subsidy on a biennial basis. Because local taxes do not support elementary and secondary public education, state revenue in Hawaii originates from the following tax sources: individual and corporate income, general sales, excise, inheritance, and miscellaneous other taxes (Bell, 2019).

County and city governments are the only entities permitted to collect property tax in Hawaii. State law additionally authorizes a hold harmless provision; thereby, each school does not receive any fewer state dollars than granted in the previous year (Brimley et al., 2020).

Hawaii's biennium budget designates funds to schools through five specific allocations, with four other allocations to fund the state education agency, charter schools, and libraries. Hawaii's modified full funding model releases monies through the EDN 100 account, which is a school fund. This fund directly distributes money to individual schools and represents 58 percent of the total general fund education budget in the 2020 fiscal year (Hawaii's Department of Education, 2019a).

The weighted student formula sets a baseline amount of money for each student in the EDN 100 school fund, with an additional sum based on varying student needs and school characteristics. Monies follow the student to their respective schools, which intends to equalize opportunities for academic student achievement (Hawaii's Department of Education, 2019b).

Every year Hawaii's Committee on Weights recommends specific student formula weights and school characteristics. Based on the school amount, each principal works closely with a site-based advisory school community council (i.e., elected teachers, noncertified staff, parents, students, and community members) to create an annual academic and financial plan. For fiscal year 2020, student formula weights and per-student allocations in the state budget were as follows (Hawaii Department of Education, 2019b):

- prekindergarten and special education (1.0 formula weight), $4,465.25;
- kindergarten–grade 2 student (1.0), $4,465.25;
- middle school student (1.0), $4,465.25;
- high school student (1.0), $4,465.25;
- kindergarten–grade 2 class size (.15), $669.79;
- middle school class size (.034), $150.00;
- English language learner (.2505), $1,118.84;
- economically disadvantaged student (.10), $446.53;
- nonproficient English language learner (.389), $1,586.65;
- limited proficient English language learner (.194), $868.04;
- fully proficient English language learner (.065), $289.35;
- transient student (.05), $223.26; and
- gifted and talented student (.265), $1,183.29.

The school characteristics with allocations per building in the 2020 fiscal year were elementary school, $307,000; middle school, $402,000; high school, $472,000; kindergarten (K)–grade 12 combination school, $750,000; K–8 combination school, $525,000; and grades 6–12 combination school, $537,000 (Hawaii Department of Education, 2019b).

The Hawaii Department of Education (2019a) explained that the EDN 150 school fund of the budget supported special education services (e.g., resources for prescriptive programs and related teaching positions) and represented 23 percent of the total budget in the 2020 fiscal year. The EDN 400 school fund financed districtwide expenses for utilities, safety, transportation, repairs, and food services. This account comprised 12 percent of the budget in the 2020 fiscal year. The EDN 500 school fund paid for community services (e.g., adult education and after-school programs) and comprised less than 1 percent of the budget in the 2020 fiscal year. The EDN 700 school fund subsidized early learning opportunities for four-year-old children, which encompassed less than 1 percent of the budget in the 2020 fiscal year.

The state department of education and other entities received the remaining 6.6 percent of the budget in the 2020 fiscal year. The EDN 200 state share was 3.4 percent of the total budget for professional development, standards implementation, and teacher licensing. The EDN 300 fund for state administration expenses (i.e., board of education and department of education) represented 3.2 percent of the entire budget. Allocations for public libraries (EDN 407) and charter schools (EDN 600) were other biennial budget amounts (Hawaii Department of Education, 2019a).

Because districts in Hawaii cannot spend more than the amount legislated by the state, the modified full state funding structure affords the funding ceiling for schools; whereas, the flat grant format in North Carolina offers the funding floor. State law in North Carolina additionally permits districts the opportunity to increase system funding with local revenue (Lincoln Institute of Land Policy, 2018).

Odden and Picus (2020) claimed that full state funding could achieve fiscal equalization with adjustments for differing student needs; however, this model obliterates local financing initiatives. By eliminating local tax efforts by communities in Hawaii's funding distribution system, school districts do not have an opportunity to increase school funding beyond the level legislated by the state.

## Foundation Model

In a conventional foundation model, the state delivers funding as basic or equalization aid. A three-step formula calculates the state's general foundation funding in a classic scheme. In step 1, the applied formula multiplies the full-time equivalent student enrollment by the legislatively set per-pupil dollar amount. The formula in step 2 multiplies a district's aggregate property assessed valuation by the state set local millage tax rate, establishing the district's local share. In step 3, the formula subtracts the general foundation aid from the local share to calculate a district's basic aid.

The foundation program intends to equalize funding between property-poor and property-rich districts. In a foundation program, a property-poor district with the same student enrollment as a property-rich district obtains proportionally more state funding than the property-rich district due to the calculated local share.

Verstegen (2018) distinguished 32 states that utilized the modified foundation model (see table 3.2). The District of Columbia also employed this model (Office of the State Superintendent of Education, 2019). The West Virginia Public School Support Program, a modified foundation model, distributed state funding with a ten-step formula to arrive at the state's basic aid for each school district (West Virginia Department of Education, 2019a).

According to the West Virginia Department of Education (2019a), Steps 1, 2, and 5 of the Public Support Allowance Program grants dollars to the 55 county school districts for full-time equivalent employee salaries (i.e., Step 1: Professional Educators, Step 2: Service Personnel, and Step 5: Professional Student Support).

The annual state statutory salary for each employee by classification and the employment experience schedule establishes the funding level by the state. In these three steps, the net enrollment—the number of full-time equivalent students (i.e., prekindergarten–grade 12)—with the ratio of employees per 1,000 students authorized by the state generates the general foundation dollars in each category. Step 3 funds the employer's benefit costs through a statutorily set amount or percentage of the employee's salary for the 2020 fiscal year:

- health insurance, average of $7,403.40 per employee approved by the state;
- social security, 7.65 percent of the state statutory salary per approved employee;
- unemployment insurance, 0.04 percent of the state statutory salary per approved employee; and
- workers' compensation, 0.82 percent of the state statutory salary per approved employee.

Step 4 funds transportation operating costs, including bus driver salaries, maintenance, bus replacement, and contract services, based on the number of net enrollment students per square miles in the service county. Step 6 accounts for general operating costs (e.g., instructional programming materials, supplies, and equipment), substitute employee costs, and the faculty senate. Step 7 offers an allowance for instructional program improvement, technology, and advanced placement programs based on set variables (West Virginia Department of Education, 2019a).

Step 8 (i.e., General Foundation Aid) sums steps 1 through 7. Step 9 subtracts each school district's local share, which is 90 percent of a district's aggregate taxable assessed valuation multiplied by the levy millage rate assigned by the state. The formula then deducts 4 percent for uncollected taxes in the district. After tabulating steps 1 through 7 and subtracting the local share plus deduction, step 10 equals the state basic aid for each school district (West Virginia Department of Education, 2019a). Figure 3.3 illustrates the

| West Virginia Public School Support Allowance | Brooke County Schools |
|---|---|
| Step 1: Professional Educators | $6,769,302 |
| Step 2: Service Personnel | $3,245,039 |
| Step 3: Employee Benefits | $1,093,441 |
| Step 4: Transportation | $1,018,590 |
| Step 5: Professional Student Support Personnel | $405,028 |
| Step 6: General Operating Costs, Substitutes, and Faculty Senates | $1,616,048 |
| Step 7: Instructional Programs | $849,345 |
| Step 8: General Foundation Aid | $17,381,181 |
| Step 9: Minus Local Share - (adjustment for uncollected tax) | - $5,682,581 - ($24,780) |
| Step 10: State Basic Aid | $11,683,840 |

**Figure 3.3.   Brooke County Schools, FY 2019-Public School Support Allowance**

*Source:* West Virginia Department of Education. (2019b). *Final computations: Public school support program for the 2018–19 year*. East Charleston, WV: Author.

West Virginia Public School Support Allowance formula and funding in the 2019 fiscal year for Brooke County Schools with a net enrollment of 2,935 full-time equivalent students.

Foundation programs possess several appealing aspects, including a structured formula that formally equalizes funding for students based on a district's fiscal capacity. Deducting an established state local tax rate (i.e., mills) in the foundation formula intends to equalize funding between property-poor and property-rich districts (Brimley et al., 2020).

Brimley et al. (2020) asserted that foundation programs apply a minimum education in terms of educational opportunities for students in poverty-poor school districts to compete with students in property-rich districts. Because foundation programs, by law, allow districts to collect a local tax above the foundation level, overall funding discrepancies can exist between per-pupil funding in poor- and rich-property districts. On another note, jurisdictions typically do not establish an adequate budget allocation for the foundation program, and the set allotment increases very slowly over time (Odden & Picus, 2020).

## Power Equalization Model

The power equalization model, based on per-pupil assessed valuation, equalizes state assistance based on the school district's ability to raise revenue instead of establishing a minimum aggregate assessed property valuation like the foundation model. However, similar to the foundation model, the power equalization model does factor a district's fiscal capacity that permits property-poor districts to receive more state aid than property-rich districts with a similar number of students (Odden & Picus, 2020).

In contrast to the foundation model, the power equalization model guarantees that all school districts receive the same revenue based on the state's average assessed valuation or tax base (Odden & Picus, 2020).

The power equalization model has three conventional derivations: percentage equalization, guaranteed tax yield, and guaranteed tax base. In a classic percentage equalization program, an aid ratio compares the district's assessed valuation to the state's average district assessed valuation. When the local school district resolves its budget, the state finances a percentage of the district budget based on the basic aid ratio.

A traditional guaranteed tax yield program ensures equal per-pupil revenue based on equal tax effort by designating an average tax yield for the state. A conventional guaranteed tax base program does not necessarily specify a minimum spending level but provides all districts with access to a state guaranteed per-pupil tax base defined as the average assessed property valuation (Odden & Picus, 2020).

For example, District A approves 10 mills, which garners $1,000 in local property tax, while 10 mills generate $5,000 of property tax in District B. When a state guarantees a $500,000 per-pupil assessed valuation (i.e., tax base), but a district has a $100,000 per-pupil tax base (District A), the state matches dollars to reach the same state equalization aid as District B with a $500,000 per-pupil tax base. As such, District A receives $4,000 in state aid per student; whereas, District B does not receive any state funding. Figure 3.4 illustrates this calculation.

Verstegen (2018) concluded that seven states employed a modified power equalization model. Wisconsin's three-tiered equalization formula, for example,

| District | Guaranteed Tax Base | Local Tax Rate | Guaranteed Revenue Per Pupil | Assessed Valuation Per Pupil | Actual Local Revenue Per Pupil | State Aid/ Pupil | Total Revenue/ Pupil |
|---|---|---|---|---|---|---|---|
| A | $500,000 | 10 mills | $5,000 | $100,000 | $1,000 | $4,000 | $5,000 |
| B | $500,000 | 10 mills | $5,000 | $500,000 | $5,000 | $0 | $5,000 |

Guaranteed Tax Base/Pupil  -  Valuation/Pupil  X  Local Tax Rate  =  State Basic Aid/Pupil

**Figure 3.4. Conventional Guaranteed Tax Base Formula**
*Source:* Author created.

shares the expenses between the state and the local district with each tier contributing a portion. State basic aid offsets disparities in districts' per-pupil assessed valuation. When a school district has a per-pupil assessed valuation below the state guaranteed assessed valuation on any of the three tiers, state basic aid grants the difference between the local per-pupil assessed valuation and the state guaranteed per-pupil assessed valuation.

According to the Wisconsin Department of Public Instruction (2019), Marshall Public School District, with 998 full-time equivalent students collected $8,135,237 in state basic aid during the 2020 fiscal year. In Wisconsin's guaranteed tax yield formula, the primary funding tier ensures that state funds are available for most school districts regardless of their assessed valuation. In this tier, the state's shared ceiling cost was $1,000 for each student, and Marshall's total primary shared cost was $1,073,000 for the 2020 fiscal year. The primary per-pupil assessed valuation state guarantee was $1,930,000 for the 2020 fiscal year. The primary net guaranteed funding was $1,620,971,748. The district's primary authorized rate was 0.0005183 of the state's primary guaranteed assessed valuation ($2,070,890,000). To calculate the dollars that the Marshall Public Schools received in primary aid for the 2020 fiscal year, the primary tier formula multiplies the primary rate (0.0005183) by the primary net guaranteed value ($1,620,971,748), totaling $839,874 in primary tier aid.

For the secondary tier, the state guaranteed per-pupil assessed valuation is lower, meaning that fewer wealthy districts obtain state basic aid in this tier. The secondary tier's state guarantee (i.e., per-student assessed valuation) was $1,299,413, and Marshall Public School District had a total secondary assessed valuation of $1,394,270,149 for the 2020 fiscal year. The district secondary tier's sanctioned rate was 0.00690543 of the state's secondary guaranteed valuation ($1,394,270,149) divided by the district's secondary shared cost ($9,628,029) for the 2020 fiscal year. To calculate the funds that Marshall Public Schools accepted in secondary tier aid, the secondary tier formula multiplies the secondary required rate (0.00690543) by the secondary net guaranteed value ($944,351,897). Marshall Public School District collected $6,521,156 in secondary tier aid for the 2020 fiscal year.

The third tier has a much lower state guaranteed assessed per-pupil valuation to ensure that high-spending districts only obtain third tier state basic aid, when districts are poor in assessed valuation. The state guaranteed assessed per-student valuation in the third tier was $621,410, and Marshall Public School District had $617,193,330 in third tier per-pupil assessed valuation for the 2020 fiscal year.

The district's tertiary rate (0.00418325) was the tertiary state guaranteed valuation ($1,267,237,205) divided by the district's third tier shared cost

($2,789,280). To calculate the revenue that Marshall Public Schools collected in the third tier for the 2020 fiscal year, this formula multiplies the tertiary approved rate (0.00409968) by the tertiary net guaranteed value ($216,854,678), which equals the tertiary state guaranteed assessed valuation ($666,772,930). Marshall Public School District collected $907,157 in third tier state aid for the 2020 fiscal year.

Marshall Public School District's total state equalization aid was the sum of all three tiers ($8,268,187) minus charter school ($133,068) and other deductions ($188), Marshall Public School District accepted $8,134,931 in state equalization aid for the 2020 fiscal year. Figure 3.5 illustrates Marshall Public School District's state equalization aid by tiers in the 2020 fiscal year.

| Primary Tier | + | Secondary Tier | + | Third Tier | - | Deductions | = | Total State Aid |
|---|---|---|---|---|---|---|---|---|
| $839,874 | + | $6,521,156 | + | $907,157 | - | $133,256 | = | $8,134,931 |

**Figure 3.5.   Marshall Public School District, FY 2020-State Equalization Aid by Tiers**
*Source:* Wisconsin Department of Public Instruction. (2019). *Certification of general aid: 2019–20- Marshall Public School District.* Madison, WI: Author.

Because community voters and school board members control local education funding, variables in the power equalization model strongly influence a district's state basic aid. With this structure, the state cannot escape its proportionate fiscal responsibility. As stated by Brimley et al. (2020), a power equalization model greatly reduces, and sometimes eliminates, a district's assessed valuation to offer a quality education for students in poor property districts unlike the foundation model. When a state simply supplies districts with an equal opportunity to fund education for district students, state basic aid rarely achieves fiscal neutrality.

## Hybrid Funding Model

To create an acceptable basic aid plan for a majority of constituents, policy makers often devise funding distribution methods that combine concepts from two or more models. Hybrid funding models synthesize the best ideas from various models by applying factors from different methodologies into a single format. Nine states utilize a hybrid design to distribute state funds (Verstegen, 2018).

Utah, for example, employs a hybrid model with a foundation concept based on a weighted student allocation and a guaranteed yield principle by assigning a statewide property tax rate. Illinois utilizes a combination of the foundation and flat grant models. Kentucky uses foundation model concepts with a guaranteed tax base format that recognizes a two-tiered adjusted tax base. Georgia, Montana, New York, Oklahoma, and Texas distribute state funds via a foundation model with power equalization principles (Verstegen, 2018).

School districts in Texas sued the state on the constitutionality of their funding model six times since the 1980s; a hybrid funding method prevailed. Proponents of the lawsuit asserted that the current system failed to grant districts with sufficient funding, produced disparities between poor- and rich-property school districts, and expected property-poor districts to locally tax properties at a higher millage rate than property-rich districts. The Texas Supreme Court in 2016 upheld the state's public school funding system (SchoolFunding.Info, 2019).

By employing concepts from the foundation and power equalization models, the Texan hybrid funding model distributes state basic aid via a two-tiered structure. The Tier I allotment, adjusted by a geographical cost-of-education index and district size, bases funding on the average daily attendance of regular, special education, vocational, bilingual, and gifted and talented students.

Tier I additionally incorporates funding for transportation, compulsory education, and specialized high school allotments. As in a foundation model, Texas school districts are responsible for a portion of the entitlement. As such, districts must subtract revenue from their Tier I allocation through a local fund assessment at the prescribed state millage rate on local property tax. When a district's revenue entitlement is less than its local fund assignment, then that district is ineligible for Tier 1 state aid, and funds raised in excess of $514,000 per weighted average daily attendance are subject to recapture, which is commonly referred to as the "Robin Hood" effect (Smith, 2017a).

Tier II releases more dollars to school districts via a guaranteed yield approach. The state guarantees each district a minimum yield on each penny of local property tax collection, using a combination of state basic aid and local revenue. When a property-poor district raises as much revenue as the tax base allows, the state bolsters the Tier II yield to the state guaranteed tax base level. Districts with a moderate property wealth that raise more local funds collect less state basic aid. Very rich property districts receive minimal, if any, Tier II state basic aid because these districts locally raise the entire guarantee (Smith, 2017a).

Figure 3.6 shows the funding for Aransas Pass Independent School District in the 2020 fiscal year with a 1,550 full-time equivalent average daily student attendance via Texas's hybrid state funding system.

| Texas Hybrid School Funding System | Aransas Pass ISD |
|---|---|
| **Tier I Allotments** | |
| Regular Program | $8,638,795 |
| Special Education | $882,703 |
| Career and Technology | $631,274 |
| Gifted and Talented | $55,102 |
| Compulsory Education | $1,645,088 |
| Bilingual Education | $74.541 |
| Transportation | $121,928 |
| Specialized High School | $107,250 |
| **Total Cost of Tier I** | $12,106,693 |
| **Minus Local Fund Assignment** | -$6,753,489 |
| **State Tier I Share** | $5,353,204 |
| **Plus State Tier II Allotment and other Program Allocations** | $1,486,993 |
| - Total Available School Fund | $418,720 |
| Tier II Allotment | $1,068,273 |
| **State Basic Aid** | $6,421,477 |

**Figure 3.6.   Aransas Pass ISD, FY 2020-Texas Hybrid Funding**
*Source:* Texas Education Agency. (2019b). *2019–20 Summary of finances. Aransas Pass ISD.* Austin, TX: Author.

As seen, each state formula can be very complex (Odden & Picus, 2020). To review a state's description of the formula, click or search for the website at https://schoolfinancesdav.wordpress.com, select a state, and investigate the formula components (Verstegen, 2018). Fortunately for school officials, the state department of education staff calculates and distributes each district's state basic aid per formula. School officials, however, should be aware of their state's basic aid formula, variables, and computations.

## CATEGORICAL AID

Although each state and the District of Columbia distribute monies to public school districts differently through unique basic aid formulas, 49 of the 50 states and the District of Columbia allot categorical aid to support specific purposes, such as special education, pupil transportation, limited English proficiency, bilingual education, and/or economic disadvantagement. When a state appropriates categorical aid above basic aid, the allotment simply grants extra monetary support for the identified student group or program (Verstegen, 2018).

Categorical funds, restricted to purposeful spending by specified category, do not equalize district fiscal capacity. With these funds distinct from basic aid, the legislature may easily track categorical allocations by line and simply reduce or eliminate these targeted monies in the jurisdiction's budget (Brimley et al., 2020).

Although each jurisdiction has unique regulations for categorical aid, pupil headcount is the most common distribution variable through entitlement formulas. Due to categorical funding's strict spending regulations, the restrictions may limit a district in delivering services beyond the guidelines (Brimley et al., 2020).

To explore categorical aid distribution means by state for transportation and small schools as well as provisions for English language learners, gifted and talented, and low-income students, click or search for the website A Quick Glance at School Finance: A 50-State Survey of School Finance Policies at https://schoolfinancesdav.wordpress.com, click a category, and review specific state data.

## SPECIAL EDUCATION FUNDING

Because students with special needs require additional resources to meet their essential educational requirements, most states offer extra financial support for special education students, programs, and services. While each state and the District of Columbia fund special education differently, jurisdictions distribute funding for special education programs and services using six distinct approaches: multiple student weights, resource-based, census-based, reimbursement, block grants, and single student weights (Education Commission of the States, 2019).

The multiple student weight (MSW) system is the most common method for distributing special education funding to districts. Sixteen states and the District of Columbia exhibit this practice (see table 3.3). For this method the funding formula assigns children with disabilities a different weight or dollar amount based on disability. In a resource-based (RB) method, seven states distribute resources in the form of staff positions based on the number of approved students who require special education services (Education of the States, 2019).

In a census-based (CB) system for eight states, the state assumes that each district has the same percentage of students who require special education services without regard to the individual student count. This method simply funds a dollar amount or weight for all children with disabilities in a district. Seven states use a reimbursement (R) method for special education funding. Districts submit actual expenditures to the state with this methodology, and the state reimburses districts for all or a portion of actual district spending (Education of the States, 2019).

In a single weight system (SWS), districts in 11 states receive additional funding for each special needs child regardless of the disability. Utah employs a block grant (BG) method in which the state distributes a comprehensive grant to the district for special education services (Education of the States, 2019).

Because of the financial burden that special education services impose on a district, 13 states supply additional funding for high-cost students. This extra funding, often coupled with another funding mechanism, offsets expensive special education expenses. Arkansas, Connecticut, and West Virginia distribute funding only for high-cost students (Education of the States, 2019).

Table 3.3 illustrates the special education funding means employed by each jurisdiction and the number of weighted student categories, when employing that particular method.

Table 3.3.  Special Education Funding Method

| Jurisdiction[a] | Special Education Funding (Weight Categories) | | | | | |
|---|---|---|---|---|---|---|
| | MSW | RB | CB | R | SWS | BG |
| Alabama | | | X | | | |
| Alaska | | | | | X[c] | |
| Arizona | X[c] (14) | | | | | |
| California | | | X | | | |
| Colorado | X (2) | | | | | |
| Delaware | | X | | | | |
| Florida | X[c] (5) | | | | | |
| Georgia | X (5) | | | | | |
| Hawaii | | X | | | | |
| Idaho | | | X | | | |
| Illinois[b] | | X | X | | | |
| Indiana | X (5) | | | | | |
| Iowa | X (3) | | | | | |
| Kansas | | | | X | | |
| Kentucky | X (3) | | | | | |
| Louisiana | | | | | X | |

*(Continued)*

# Table 3.3. Special Education Funding Method *(Continued)*

| Jurisdiction[a] | Special Education Funding (Weight Categories) | | | | | |
|---|---|---|---|---|---|---|
| | MSW | RB | CB | R | SWS | BG |
| Maine | X[c] (2) | | | | | |
| Maryland | | | | | X | |
| Massachusetts | | | X[c] | | | |
| Michigan | | | | X | | |
| Minnesota[b] | X (3) | | | X | | |
| Mississippi | | X | | | | |
| Missouri | | | | | X | |
| Montana | | | X | | | |
| Nebraska | | | | X | | |
| Nevada | | | | | X | |
| New Hampshire | | | | | X[c] | |
| New Jersey | | | X[c] | | | |
| New Mexico | X (4) | | | | | |
| New York | | | | | X | |
| North Carolina | | | | | X | |
| North Dakota | | | | | X | |
| Ohio | X (6) | | | | | |
| Oklahoma | X (10) | | | | | |
| Oregon | | | | | X | |
| Pennsylvania | X (3) | | | | | |
| Rhode Island | | | | X[c] | | |
| South Carolina | X (5) | | | | | |
| South Dakota[b] | X (6) | | X | | | |
| Tennessee | | X | | | | |
| Texas | X (6) | | | | | |
| Utah | | | | | | X |
| Vermont | | X[c] | | | | |
| Virginia | | X | | | | |
| Washington | | | | | X | |
| Washington, DC | X (5) | | | | | |
| Wisconsin | | | | X[c] | | |
| Wyoming | | | | X | | |

*Source:* Education Commission of the States (2019).
*Notes:* [a]Arkansas, Connecticut, and West Virginia are not listed in the table because these states only provide funding for high-cost students. [b]This state uses a hybrid method from two methodologies. [c]This state also funds high special education costs.

## FUNDING BEYOND BASIC AND CATEGORICAL AID

The majority of jurisdiction education funds flow through basic and categorical aid allotments. States and the District of Columbia (i.e., jurisdictions) occasionally offer supplementary monies to public school districts by approval from the legislature through entitlements and/or discretionary grants. Entitlements and discretionary grants often incentivize districts toward specific action, although schools regularly spend above the grant monies on initiatives (Odden & Picus, 2020).

After-school programs; preschool services; school safety; parental involvement; reading literacy; science, technology, engineering, and math (STEM) initiatives; and community services; as well as bullying, dropout, and substance abuse prevention services are popular projects funded by entitlements or competitive measures.

Entitlement (noncompetitive) grants allot funds to grantees with a formula usually prescribed by legislation or regulation. Applicants do not compete for these funds; they become automatically eligible for the dollars when meeting fixed factors, such as student enrollment or district wealth characteristics (e.g., per capita income). For example, each public school in North Carolina acquired a per-pupil entitlement grant to purchase school technology, panic alarms, or connectivity and/or to fund middle school safety officers (North Carolina Department of Public Instruction, 2019a).

The Vermont Tobacco Litigation Fund supported tobacco prevention activities and dispersed entitled funding based on student enrollment (Vermont Agency of Education, 2019). The Indian Education for All grants, a state entitlement program in Montana, appropriated dollars for each identified Native American child in eligible school districts; this entitlement intended to close the educational achievement gap between Native American children and students from other ethnic origins (Montana Office of Public Instruction, 2019).

Jurisdictions also may bestow discretionary (competitive) grants to school districts by application with a formal review and evaluation. The awards are available outside basic aid and often encourage innovative programs based on specific criteria. For instance, the Family, Career, and Consumer Leaders of America discretionary grant in New Jersey funded one application in the 2019 fiscal year with a continuation for the 2020 fiscal year. The purpose of this grant was to prepare students for careers in human services. The state allotted $146,500 in the state budget for this initiative (State of New Jersey Department of Education, 2019).

Entitlements and/or competitive grants often become nonexistent when educational funding is tight. To become aware of a jurisdiction's grant opportunities, visit the jurisdiction's department of education website, which typically maintains a list of available grants with application and submission guidelines. Chapter 4 discusses the competitive grant application process in detail.

## FUNDING FOR NONPUBLIC AND
## PUBLIC CHARTER SCHOOLS

### Nonpublic Schools

Numerous legal actions over the years prevented jurisdictions from funding nonpublic schools, although states and the District of Columbia permit public dollars for nonpublic school students in limited circumstances. In *Everson v. Board of Education* (1947), the U.S. Supreme Court upheld public subsidies for student transportation to nonpublic schools as a benefit to children. This case authorized public transportation for nonpublic school students. The Tenth Amendment authorizes jurisdictional decisions to grant or deny permission of public funds for transportation privileges for nonpublic students.

The Office of Innovation and Improvement (2019a) reported that 22 states entitled nonpublic school students public transportation privileges similar to those afforded public school students. Of further note, Ohio nonpublic parents or guardians may accept a state payment in lieu of public transportation in accordance with Ohio Revised Code 3327.02, when the local board of education finds the child impractical to transport (Ohio Department of Education, 2019b).

Eleven states and the District of Columbia grant wide discretion for public schools to arrange nonpublic school students' transportation without cost. State law in Kentucky and a Missouri Supreme Court decision expressly prohibits public school funds for nonpublic student transportation. By Attorney General Opinion in Oklahoma, public school buses cannot transport students to nonpublic schools. Fourteen states do not hold a state policy about transporting nonpublic school students via public support (Office of Innovation and Improvement, 2019a).

Secular textbooks have been another hotly contested issue. In *Board of Education v. Allen* (1968), the U.S. Supreme Court upheld a New York law that ordered public schools to lend textbooks to private schools without charge because the books contained nonreligious content. In *Mitchell v. Helms* (2000), the U.S. Supreme Court held that using government funds to purchase instructional materials and equipment for nonpublic school students did not violate the Establishment Clause (Alexander & Alexander, 2019).

According to the Office of Innovation and Improvement (2019a), 19 states and the District of Columbia do not regulate the use of public funds for nonpublic school textbooks or materials. Twelve states have permissive laws to borrow textbooks at no cost, purchase textbooks, or use available surplus books from public schools.

California allows nonpublic schools to order state adopted materials. Maryland's Nonpublic Student Textbook allocation grants direct state funding to nonpublic schools for loaned textbooks, computer hardware, and software. Illinois specifies a state block grant to nonpublic schools for secular textbook purchases. Indiana students who attend nonpublic schools may receive reimbursement payments from the state for textbooks, while public schools in Louisiana may request administrative costs and reimbursement from the state for nonpublic school textbooks (Office of Innovation and Improvement, 2019a).

Seven states allow local school boards to loan textbooks and instructional materials to nonpublic school students upon request. Five states deem the use of public school funds for secular textbooks unconstitutional by state law or court decision. The Oklahoma attorney general issued an opinion that public funds should not purchase nonpublic school textbooks (Office of Innovation and Improvement, 2019a).

In *Zobrest v. Catalina Foothills School District* (1993), the U.S. Supreme Court overturned prior law on government spending for auxiliary services to private schools and students. This case allowed government funding for certain services based on student need. In this case, a student's residential school did not matter (Alexander & Alexander, 2019).

Twenty-six states and the District of Columbia grant public funding to nonpublic school students for miscellaneous assistances, although 24 states do not permit such spending in nonpublic schools. The Office of Innovation and Improvement (2019a) reported that school districts and county health departments in seven states and the District of Columbia must offer auxiliary health services to children attending nonpublic schools in the same manner delivered to public school students. Nonpublic schools and parents in another seven states may request participation in the school health services program.

Seven states and the District of Columbia award public monies to nonpublic schools for testing; two states approve funding to nonpublic school students for driver's education; and seven states authorize public monies to nonpublic school staff for professional development. North Carolina's nonpublic schools may apply for a grant from the Office of Mental Health to identify and treat adolescents at risk of suicide (Office of Innovation and Improvement, 2019).

Nonpublic schools in Massachusetts may apply for state grants to fund science, technology, engineering, and mathematics instruction. New Hampshire grants state aid to nonpublic schools for technology, and Illinois offers nonpublic schools state loans for technology. Ohio and Louisiana reimburse nonpublic schools for nonreligious functions though auxiliary funding. Texas law permits public schools to provide crossing guard funds to nonpublic schools (Office of Innovation and Improvement, 2019a). To view jurisdiction funding and regulations for nonpublic schools by state, click or search for the U.S. Department of Education website at https://www2.ed.gov/about/inits/ed/non-public-education/regulation-map/index.html.

In a dramatic shift in federal policy, the U.S. Supreme Court in *Zelman v. Simmons-Harris* (2002) upheld public monies for parochial schools and nonpublic schoolchildren through voucher programs referred to as scholarships. By a 5–4 vote, the High Court ruled that Ohio's program was constitutional under the principle of "true private choice." This opinion advanced state funded scholarships for student tuition at private schools (Alexander & Alexander, 2019).

Vouchers give parents the freedom to choose a private school for their children, using public funding for their children's education. Under such a program, funds typically expended by a school district would be allocated to a participating family in the form of a voucher to pay partial or full tuition for their child's private school, including religious and nonreligious options (EdChoice, 2019).

The District of Columbia and 15 states (Arkansas, Florida, Georgia, Indiana, Louisiana, Maine, Maryland, Mississippi, New Hampshire, North Carolina, Ohio, Oklahoma, Utah, Vermont, and Wisconsin) grant vouchers. Eleven of these states do not have an income limit for participation. Nine programs restrict participation to special needs children. When a Vermont or Maine district does not have an available public school, the district voters may approve a public voucher for nonpublic school tuition (EdChoice, 2019; Erwin, 2019). To examine specific state information on vouchers, click or search for the EdChoice resource at https://www.edchoice.org/wp-content/uploads/2019/01/The-ABCs-of-School-Choice-2019-Edition.pdf.

Tax credit scholarships that offer private school scholarships for tuition, fees, and other related services allow taxpayers to receive full or partial tax credits when they donate to nonpublic schools. Eligible taxpayers in 18 states may include individuals and businesses. Alabama, Arizona, Georgia, Illinois, Indiana, Montana, Nevada, Oklahoma, South Carolina, and Virginia permit individuals and corporations to claim a tax credit for eligible student scholarships. Iowa and Louisiana grant individuals a tax credit; whereas, Florida, Kansas, New Hampshire, Pennsylvania, Rhode Island, and South Dakota sanction businesses to apply for a tax credit with scholarships awarded to qualified students (EdChoice, 2019).

## Public Charter Schools

Funding for public charter schools varies significantly among the District of Columbia and 44 states that permit such schools; however, each jurisdiction with a charter law grants state funding for public charter schools. Similar to public school funding, a combination of jurisdiction and local dollars fund public charter schools. Legislatures across the country designated three different charter school funding processes (Education Commission of the States, 2018b).

To establish basic aid for charter schools in 31 states, the per-pupil revenue from authorizers (e.g., public school district, higher education institute, state board of education, nonprofit organization, charter board commission, or municipal government) regulates the monies. With this method, the jurisdiction releases the basic aid to the charter school from the department of education to the authorizer (Education Commission of the States, 2018b).

Per-pupil revenue from the school district in which the student resides is another strategy that eight states employ to establish charter school state basic aid. As such, a charter school could accept differing amounts of money for students from different districts. In this system, the state distributes the dollars to the school district or charter authorizer who reallocates the funds to the charter school (Education Commission of the States, 2018b).

As a third means, a statewide average per-pupil allocation establishes the state aid in Arkansas, Hawaii, Idaho, and Minnesota with the school district, state, or authorizer releasing the funds. In the District of Columbia, the city government distributes the charter monies based on a unit funding formula similar to traditional public schools (Education Commission of the States, 2018b). To examine basic aid regulations and organizations that actually disburse the basic aid to charter schools, click or search for the Education Commission of the States website at http://ecs.force.com/mbdata/mbquestNB2C?rep=CS1716. To study specific funding distributions for public charter schools, click or search for the website A Quick Glance at School Finance: A 50-State Survey of School Finance Policies at https://schoolfinancesdav.wordpress.com, click a state, and investigate charter school funding.

Besides basic aid, states and the District of Columbia also apportion categorical aid to charter schools. For this funding, the jurisdiction assigns the monies similar to traditional schools in two major classifications—transportation and special education. Although state law in most states does not mandate transportation services for charter school students, many states grant transportation funding for these students (Education Commission of the States, 2018a). To view a jurisdiction's basic and categorical aid regulations for charter schools, click or search for the Education Commission of the States website at http://ecs.force.com/mbdata/mbquestNB2C?rep=CS1716. To see data on transporting charter school students by jurisdiction, click or search for the Education Commission of the States website at http://ecs.force .com/mbdata/mbquestNB2C?rep=CS1707.

States and the District of Columbia allocate the majority of charter school special education funding through an established basic aid explained earlier in this chapter. However, the Education Commission of the States (2018) specified that some states deliver supplementary special education funding to charter schools through categorical aid.

Charter schools in Georgia, Idaho, Illinois, Indiana, Kansas, Maryland, Michigan, Missouri, Nevada, New Hampshire, New Jersey, Ohio, South Carolina, Tennessee, Texas, Wisconsin, and Wyoming may qualify for categorical aid to offset the cost of educating students with high-cost, low-incidence disabilities. To view categorical aid regulations for charter schools by jurisdiction, click or search for the Education Commission of the States website at http://ecs.force.com/mbdata/mbquestNB2C?rep=CS1716.

## SUMMARY

States and the District of Columbia finance specific programs and services for their residents. In order to fund elementary and secondary public education, jurisdictions primarily rely on income and sales tax; some states also levy statewide property tax and other assorted taxes to fund public education. Nontax sources are available in a few jurisdictions.

Legislatures authorize the distribution method and educational funding level in accordance with budgetary procedures. Each state and the District of Columbia hold a unique structure for distributing jurisdiction funding to school districts, which may include a flat grant, full state funding, modified foundation, hybrid, or modified power equalization processes. The basic aid formula can be complex. States and the District of Columbia may allocate additional funding through categorical aid, entitlements, or discretionary grants. Jurisdictions may also authorize funding to nonpublic and charter schools. Charter school basic and categorical aid formulas across the country are as complex as traditional public education funding processes.

## PROJECTS

1. Conduct an internet search to identify the revenue sources in your jurisdiction and list the top two income bases for public services.

2. Conduct an internet search to discover the general fund spending in your jurisdiction and relate expenditure percentages by service category.

3. Describe and state your jurisdiction's budget processes, including the fiscal year arrangement, activity timeframe, and primary budget approaches from the *Budget Processes in the States* at https://www.nasbo.org/reports-data/budget-processes-in-the-states.

4. Study and report a basic aid formula for fund distribution to public schools and the categorical funding by clicking or searching for a state from the website A Quick Glance at School Finance: A 50-State Survey of School Finance Policies at https://schoolfinancesdav.wordpress.com.

5. Conduct an internet search of your jurisdiction's department of education to investigate and explain the entitlement and discretionary grants available to schools.

6. Identify and record the funding for a charter school by clicking or searching for a state from the website A Quick Glance at School Finance: A 50-state Survey of School Finance Policies at https://schoolfinancesdav.wordpress.com.

7. Identify and report the jurisdiction funding for a nonpublic school by clicking or searching on the U.S. Department of Education website at https://www2.ed.gov/about/inits/ed/non-public-education/regulation-map/index.html.

*Chapter Four*

# Federal Revenue

## OBJECTIVES

After reading this chapter, you should be able to

✓ describe the federal budget process (NELP 5.3, 6.1, 6.2, 6.3);
✓ comprehend federal entitlement funding by program and discretionary grants (NELP 5.3, 6.1, 6.2, 6.3); and
✓ understand the grant writing process and apply for funding (NELP 1.2, 4.1, 4.2, 4.3, 4.4, 5.2, 6.1, 6.2, 6.3).

Federal government revenue supplies a minor portion of elementary and secondary public schools' financial support, especially when compared with state and local revenue. The federal government's share of combined public school funding averaged around 7.8 percent from 2014 to 2019 (see table 1.1), due in part to the U.S. Constitution's Tenth Amendment (Alexander & Alexander, 2019). The federal government granted 7.3 percent of the entire elementary and secondary revenue as a national average in fiscal year 2019 (National Education Association, 2019b).

A school administrator should be fully aware of each federal program's structure because programs may be under that individual's supervision. With an understanding of each program's spending allowances, public, nonpublic, and charter school administrators will be able to utilize each fund in the best interest of the students and staff, maximize overall school fiscal efficiency, and remain lawful with program assurances.

Monies flowing into the U.S. Treasury originate from various taxing sources. The Center on Budget and Policy Priorities (2019b) asserted federal revenue from taxes surpassed $3.3 trillion in fiscal year 2018, which represents the most current year available at the time of publication. Individual income tax comprised 51 percent of the entire federal revenue; payroll tax on workers' wages from Social Security, Medicare, and unemployment insurance was 35 percent; and corporate income tax, 6 percent. Other U.S. tax revenue from excise, estate, and other taxes comprised 8 percent of the full share for the 2018 fiscal year. (Note: The individual income tax percentage increased 4 percent in fiscal year 2018 from fiscal year 2017, and the corporate income tax percentage declined 5 percent in fiscal year 2018 from fiscal year 2017.)

The Center on Budget and Policy Priorities (2019c) reported the federal government spent $4.1 trillion in fiscal year 2018 on three basic categories— mandatory spending, 61.9 percent of all spending in the United States; discretionary defense costs, 15.7 percent; discretionary nondefense expenses, 14.7 percent; and debt interest, 7.7 percent. Social Security, a program based on eligibility criteria, expended 24.5 percent of all mandatory spending. Medicare and Medicaid subsidies were 24 percent of obligatory expenses. The 7.7 percent national debt interest denoted government payments to individuals, businesses, and foreign banks for money obligated by U.S. Treasury bills, notes, and savings bonds.

Of the $4.1 trillion spent in fiscal year 2018, the United States government financed over $3.3 trillion by federal taxation. The $540 billion in nondefense discretionary spending consisted of transportation, 4 percent of the entire spending; education, 3 percent; science and medical research, 2 percent; international affairs, 1 percent; and all other discretionary expenses, 4.7 percent. As noted, education expenditures from federal revenue hold a very modest portion of the entire federal government spending (Center on Budget and Policy Priorities, 2019c).

## BUDGET PROCESS

The Congressional Budget and Impoundment Control Act (1974) outlined the formal framework and timeline to develop the national budget for discretionary spending. An annual legislative act establishes specific appropriations. In contrast, the legislature, by law, allocates spending on mandatory programs (e.g., Social Security) as opposed to the discretionary budgetary process. Because mandatory subsidies fund specific eligibilities, recipients automatically collect dollars unless the U.S. Congress enacts new legislation to change a program (Congressional Research Service, 2019c).

The discretionary budget cycle begins with the formation of the president's budget proposal and concludes with an audit and review of expenditures. The Center on Budget and Policy Priorities (2019a) explained that guidance from the Office of Management and Budget to agencies like the U.S. Department of Education starts the budget process.

Agency officials develop budget requests during the spring into the summer and submit their initial proposed budget by early fall. The Office of Management and Budget staff reviews agency budget proposals from October to December in relation to presidential priorities, program performances, and fiscal constraints (Center on Budget and Policy Priorities, 2019a).

Based on the Office of Management recommendations, the president and staff submit the proposed presidential budget to the U.S. Congress by the first Monday in February. Twelve separate House and Senate Subcommittees on Appropriations (e.g., Labor, Health and Human Services, Education, and Related Agencies; Defense; and Homeland Security) hold hearings from February through April to question agency personnel about funding requests. Budget resolution adoptions occur in May (Center on Budget and Policy Priorities, 2019a).

Each bill independently proceeds to the House and Senate floors for amendments after the subcommittees pass their resolutions. A House-Senate conference committee then resolves differences between the separate House and Senate versions by August. Upon concurrence, the House and Senate jointly pass the agreed upon budget bill (Center on Budget and Policy Priorities, 2019a).

The president may sign or veto the budget bill. When approved into law by the president, the Office of Management and Budget appropriates authorized funds to agencies by September 10. The approved education funds flow from the U.S. Treasury to the U.S. Department of Education for the fiscal year that starts on October 1 and concludes on September 30. Legislators do not always adhere to the suggested dates, and on occasion, schools do not collect their federal dollars until after October 1 (Center on Budget and Policy Priorities, 2019a).

U.S. Department of Agriculture designated staff members oversee subsidies for other education activities, such as the National School Lunch Program. After the fiscal year ends, the General Accounting Office staff conducts an audit and expenditure review (Center on Budget and Policy Priorities, 2019a).

To apply for entitled federal funding, each state education agency (SEA), commonly known as the state department of education, submits a consolidated state plan to the U.S. Department of Education. A comprehensive set of assurances accompanies the application for guaranteed adherence to the Elementary and Secondary Education Act and administrative regulations in each Title program (Center on Standards and Assessment Implementation, 2019).

According to the U.S. Department of Education (2019c), the legislature authorizes funds to eligible recipients via formula grants based on complex mathematical equations and statistical criteria. Allocation formulas hold one or more factors (i.e., population, eligibility threshold, state average per-pupil expenditure, hold harmless provision, equity, effort, and allotment ratios for the SEA and local education agencies). Detailed formulas, by law, designate the specific amount of funds awarded to SEAs, local education agencies (LEAs), or other entities to implement each program's purpose. Federal and state staffs generate funding for each program based on data from the National Center for Education Statistics and the U.S. Census Bureau.

Once the U.S. Department of Education distributes formula grant allocations to each state agency, SEAs may retain a portion of authorized federal funds for statewide activities in accord with the State and Local Transferability Act (2015). The SEA staff representatives then distribute funds based on the U.S. Department of Education guidelines and calculations through subgrants to LEAs, generally recognized as school districts.

State and local education agencies' personnel who petition entitlement funds must assure that each formula grant is implemented as mandated, and monies must supplement—not supplant—other federal, state, or local funding already assigned for related purposes (U.S. Department of Education, 2019c).

## ENTITLEMENT GRANTS

Every Student Succeeds Act (2015), the current reauthorization of the Elementary and Secondary Education Act (1965), sanctioned seven categorically funded Title entitlement (i.e., formula) grants to assist in educating eligible student populations. U.S. Congress passed legislation in 2017 to revise Every Student Succeeds Act's accountability regulation. The 2020 fiscal year appropriations increased federal discretionary funding for Every Student Succeeds Act to $75.9 billion, which is $4.4 billion over the 2019 appropriation (House Committee on Appropriations, 2019).

The president's budget recommendation to U.S. Congress proposed eliminating funding for Title II, Title IV, and Title VI, Part A, Subpart 1 along with 26 other programs; however, all programs were reinstituted in the House Committee Appropriations (House Committee on Appropriations, 2019; U.S. Department of Education, 2019a).

Other legislation authorizing entitlement grants for primary and secondary public and nonpublic schools include the Individuals with Disabilities Education Act (1990), Child Nutrition Act (1966), Telecommunications Act (1996), Perkins Career and Technical Education Act (2006), and the Medicare Catastrophic Coverage Act of 1988 (Alexander & Alexander, 2019).

## Title I

Title I, Part A—Improving Basic Programs delivers financial assistance to schools for children aged 5 to 17 (i.e., eligible school-age population) to improve academic skills in reading and mathematics. According to the U.S. Department of Education (2018a), the U.S. Congress allocates funds through four separate statutory formulas:

- Basic grants fund LEAs when the population of economically disadvantaged school-aged children, in accord with U.S. Census Bureau data, numbers at least 10 students or the sum of eligible children exceeds 2 percent (i.e., eligibility threshold) of the total school-age population in the local education agency.
- Concentration grants stipulate additional funding for LEAs with extraordinarily large populations with more than 6,500 economically disadvantaged school-aged children or the number of eligible children exceeds 15 percent of the total school-age population in the LEA.
- Targeted grants ensure that the greatest proportion of funding reach LEAs with the largest number of economically disadvantaged school-aged children. To qualify for a Targeted grant, the number of eligible children in the LEA must exceed more than 38.24 percent of the total school-age population in the LEA.
- Education Finance Incentive grants distribute extra funds to LEAs based on the state's equity and effort factors.

Upon receipt of the LEA notification for Title I funding, the district staff selects which buildings garner funding, and the school staff decides which students qualify for Title I services.

Part A funding educates students, regardless of family income, recognized as failing or at risk of failing to meet the state's reading and mathematics standards. An eligible school may deliver services either in a targeted assistance or schoolwide program. A targeted assistance program delivers Title I services for pinpointed students outside the regular classroom. When at least 40 percent of a school's students reside with low-income families based on U.S. Census Bureau data, a schoolwide program may educate all the school's students within regular classes. Upon eligibility for targeted assistance or schoolwide programming, the school staff may elect the service delivery method (U.S. Department of Education, 2018a; Virginia Department of Education, 2018).

Part A allowable expenditures associated with the delivery of Title I targeted assistance or schoolwide programs are program related employee salaries and fringe benefits, educational materials and supplies, online courseware, equipment, and professional development (Virginia Department of Education, 2018).

To calculate LEA and SEA Title I, Part A allocations, the U.S. Department of Education utilizes recent U.S. Census Bureau data to apportion the eligible school-age population, family income estimates, and LEA boundaries. Each year the U.S. Department of Education issues a memorandum to Title I state directors advising them to review statewide Census Bureau data, verify the accuracy of school district boundaries in the state, and share the information with LEA officials statewide. SEA and LEA officials may contest data correctness (Rooney, 2018). State and district officials should participate in the data review to avoid loss of Title revenue.

With the U.S. Department of Education notification, the Census Bureau establishes a challenge period for SEA and LEA officials to question the data and request corrections. Errors by the Census Bureau generally emanate from data preparation in defining school district boundaries or the processing as well as data input for financial estimates. State and district federal program administrators generally realize formula computations, review Census Bureau data, and challenge information when necessary (Rooney, 2018). To investigate each Title I, Part A formula allocation for SEAs and LEAs, click or search for https://www.everycrsreport.com/reports/RL34721.html#_Toc252438487.

For most administrators, a thorough understanding of the formulas may be unnecessary because the staffs at the federal and state departments of education calculate and distribute funds based on the formula variables. School officials, however, should challenge the accuracy of the school-aged economically disadvantaged children population, family income estimates, and school boundary data when necessary.

The Title I, Part C—Education of Migratory Children Program stipulates formula grants to SEAs for establishing or improving education programs designed to meet learning needs for qualified children of migratory agricultural workers or fishers. The U.S. Department of Education (2019b) funds SEAs through a statutory formula based on a state's acknowledged migrant students aged 3 to 21 and the number of migrant children in summer or intersession services compared with the eligible migrant children population nationwide (i.e., state allocation ratio).

To distinguish a subgrant allocation, the SEA staff may use a formula, negotiation, or combination approach. SEA staff members in the formula approach verify the SEA migrant funding allotment for subgrants, count the eligible school-aged migrant population in each LEA, and calculate each ratio of funding for the LEAs based on the entire state allocation. SEA staff members then compute the subgrantee's share based on the LEA allocation ratio and appropriates the funds (U.S. Department of Education, 2019b).

In the negotiation approach, the SEA staff reviews LEA applications with activity descriptions and budget requests. The SEA staff regulates the subgrant allocation based on the application's quality. In the combination approach, SEA reviewers establish the LEA allocation founded on the application and the subgrant formula allocation. Allowable expenditures for related actions include student support services, parental involvement activities, before- and after-school tutoring, and professional development targeted to assist the staff in understanding and responding to the needs of migrant children (Gillette & Meyertholen, n.d.). To examine the Title I, Part C SEA and LEA allocation formulas, click or search for https://www.everycrsreport.com/reports/RL34721.html#_Toc252438496.

## Title II

Title II, Part A—Supporting Effective Instruction Program pinpoints SEA funding to prepare, train, and recruit high-quality educators for students from low-income families and minorities (National Education Association, 2019a). According to the National Association of Secondary School Administrators (2019a), Title II, Part A subgrants incentivize school districts to employ innovative methods to enhance teacher and leader quality for increased student success.

According to the Virginia Department of Education (2018), authorized spending supports

- teacher and school leader preparation academies to serve high-need schools;
- diverse workforce actions across the career continuum from teacher recruitment, employment, and retention;
- residency programs (e.g., mentoring) for teachers and school leaders;
- expansion of alternative routes to state certification, especially in states with an educator shortage in recognized academic subjects;
- rigorous, transparent, and fair evaluation systems; and
- professional development activities for educators to close achievement gaps.

## Title III

Title III, Part A—English Language Acquisition, Language Enhancement, and Academic Achievement Program aims to ensure that English language learners and immigrant students achieve at high levels in academic subjects to meet state standards. A number of permissible activities encompass bettering the instruction of English learners; acquiring or developing educational technology and accessing electronic networks; administering English language proficiency assessments; conducting community participation programs, family literacy services, and parent outreach and training (National Association of Secondary School Administrators, 2019b; National Education Association, 2019a).

Authorized spending comprises expenditures to enrich the instructional program by identifying, acquiring, and upgrading curricula, instructional materials, educational software, and assessment procedures; enhancing instruction through staff training and technology; and offering community participation and parent/family outreach programs (Virginia Department of Education, 2018). To understand the Title III, Part A SEA and LEA allocation formulas, click or search for https://www.everycrsreport.com/reports/RL34721.html#_Toc252438504.

## Title IV

Title IV, Part A—Student Support and Academic Enrichment Program subsidizes pursuits to create a well-rounded education, strengthens school conditions for student learning, and advances the effective use of technology. Each SEA obtains a Title IV, Part A allocation upon application to the U.S. Department of Education from a block grant based on the state's Title I, Part A allocation (National Education Association, 2019a; U.S. Department of Education, 2019c).

The National Association of Secondary School Administrators (2019c) reported that the Title IV, Part A specifically authorizes functions that

- provide students with a well-rounded education (e.g., science, technology, engineering, and mathematics initiatives; college and career counseling; and arts, civics, international baccalaureate, and advanced placement programs);
- support safe and healthy students through mental health counseling, drug deterrence actions, violence prevention pursuits, trauma trainings, and physical education/health activities and
- reinforce the effective use of technology with professional development for staff to implement blended instruction and classroom usage of digital devices.

Allowable expenditures may consist of expenses for accelerated and blended learning courses, bullying and drug prevention programs, technology equipment, software applications, digital resources, professional development on violence prevention, and personnel salaries to execute related programs and services (Virginia Department of Education, 2018).

Title IV, Part B—21st Century Learning Community Center Program implements academic enrichment activities for children in academically low-performing schools. Each state obtains a 21st Century Community Learning Center grant equal to its proportional share (i.e., SEA allocation ratio) of complete funding under Title I, Part A. The SEA personnel awards LEA monies by statewide competitions for allowable activities. Local grant recipients may spend the dollars on activities to promote parental involvement, library services, tutors, and technology projects (National Association of Secondary School Administrators, 2019c; National Education Association, 2019a).

## Title V

Title V, Part B—Rural Education Achievement Program addresses the unique needs of rural school districts that frequently lack the personnel and resources to compete effectively for federal discretionary grants. Title V, Part B also offers funding to districts when formula grant allocations are too meager to meet the intended purposes (National Education Association, 2019a; U.S. Department of Education, 2018c).

This entitlement comprises two formula grant programs: Small, Rural School Achievement, Subpart 1 with grants awarded directly to eligible LEAs; and Rural, Low-Income School, Subpart 2 with grants awarded to SEAs to offer subgrants to LEAs. Qualified LEAs may be eligible for both programs, and districts may use these monies to support other Title programs (U.S. Department of Education, 2018c).

Subpart 1, the Small, Rural School Achievement Program serves LEAs with fewer than 600 students in the average daily attendance (U.S. Department of Education, 2018b). Eligible districts must apply annually through Grants.gov, explained later in the chapter.

Subpart 2, the Rural, Low-Income School Program supplies rural districts with financial assistance for initiatives aimed at enhancing student achievement. The U.S. Department of Education distributes annual awards to SEAs that apply and meet requirements (U.S. Department of Education, 2018c).

The SEA staff decides which districts will obtain local subgrant allotments. Some states regulate LEA allocations on a competitive basis; other states award monies by formula. Districts may spend dollars from the Title V, Part B, Subpart 2 grant for teacher recruitment and retention, professional development, educational technology, and parental involvement (U.S. Department of Education, 2018c). To investigate the Title V, Part B, Subpart 1 SEA and LEA allocation formulas, click or search for https://www.everycrsreport .com/reports/RL34721.html#_Toc252438509. To check the Title V, Part B, Subpart 2 SEA and LEA allocation formulas, click or search for https://www .everycrsreport.com/reports/RL34721.html#_Toc252438510.

## Title VI

Title VI, Part A, Subpart 1—Indian Education Formula Grants to Local Educational Agencies focuses on the unique cultural, language, and related academic needs of American Indian and Native Alaskan students, including preschool children (Indian Education Formula Grants to Local Educational Agencies, 2017; National Education Association, 2019a).

Entitled LEAs with at least 10 eligible students enrolled in the LEA or more than 25 percent of the total student population may apply to the U.S. Department of Education. The formula establishes the LEA allocation by multiplying the number of eligible LEA students (i.e., American Indian or Native Alaskan) by an expenditure factor for the LEA grant variable. The formula divides this variable by the total of all LEA grant variables in the nation to specify an LEA allotment ratio. To calculate the LEA allocation, the formula multiplies the LEA allotment ratio by the annual Congressional Title VI allocation (Indian Education Formula Grants to Local Educational Agencies, 2017).

## Title VII

Title VII—Impact Aid affords financial assistance to local school districts that lost property tax revenue due to the presence of tax-exempt federal property (Section 7002) or experienced increased expenditures due to the enrollment of federally connected children (Section 7003b). Districts that accept Impact Aid may use the funds in whatever manner they choose in accordance with local and state requirements. School districts use Impact Aid for a wide variety of expenses, including the salaries of teachers and teacher aides; textbooks, computers, and other equipment purchases; after-school programs and remedial tutoring; advanced placement classes; special enrichment programs; and capital expenditures. Payments for children with disabilities (Section 7003d, however, must be used for the extra costs of educating federally connected children (U.S. Department of Education, 2017).

## Title VII, Subtitle B

Title VII, Subtitle B under the McKinney-Vento Homeless Assistance Act—Education for Homeless Children and Youth Program awards SEA grants, by formula, based on state allocations under Title I, Part A. Monies address the challenges that youth in homeless circumstances face in enrolling, attending, and succeeding in school. Providing technical assistance to school districts, implementing the state's McKinney-Vento plan, or awarding subgrants to LEAs are allowable usages of the state funds (National Education Association, 2019a; U.S. Department of Education, 2018b).

When the state staff chooses to offer subgrants, they must be competitive with prioritization based on need. A subgrant may support tutoring and mentoring activities; medical, dental, or mental health services; student evaluations; staff sensitivity trainings; or student transportation (U.S. Department of Education, 2018b).

## Education of School-Aged Children with Disabilities Grant, Part B

The Education of School-Aged Children with Disabilities Grant, Part B, Section 611, reauthorized in 1990, 2004, and 2015 from the initial Education for All Handicapped Children Act (1975), reinforces instructional programs, services, and materials for children aged 5 to 21 with special needs.

The Congressional Research Service (2019d) reported that SEA personnel may reserve a portion of the Part B, Section 611 allocation for statewide activities; however, they must apportion most of the allocation to LEAs.

The Part B, Section 619—Preschool Grants authorizes funding to states for programs serving children with special needs aged three to five. Part B, Sections 611 and 619 monies must supplement overall district special education spending as opposed to supplant state and local dollars. Part B funds, therefore, must pay for the excess costs of implementing special education and related services (Congressional Research Service, 2019d).

Allowable personnel expenditures in Section 611 and 619 programs include associated special education personnel salaries and fringe benefits as well as related professional development activities. Program related administrative salaries and benefits, evaluation delivery, parent involvement activities, physical plant costs, and transportation services (e.g., related bus driver salaries and benefits; adapted lifts and ramps; vehicle purchases, leases, insurances, and repairs; and contracted services) represent approved special education management excess costs.

Computer hardware, software, and peripherals for delivering special education services; assistive technology equipment; and related resources to support program implementation characterize approved instructional expenses (Congressional Research Service, 2019d). Each state department of education website typically announces allowable costs for Part B entitlement grants. To discover the Part B grant formula for SEA allocations, click or search for https://www.everycrsreport.com/reports/R44624.html#_Toc526353911. To view the Part B formula for LEA allocations, click or search for https://www.everycrsreport.com/reports/R44624.html#_Toc526353915.

## School Meal Programs

The Agriculture Adjustment Act (1935) approved the nation's initial school meal program and food commodity distributions to schools from the U.S.

Department of Agriculture. This act intended to relieve the devastating national economic recession by boosting the agricultural workforces' purchasing power, raising farmers' revenue, and offering emergency relief with respect to farmers' indebtedness.

The National School Lunch Program, established by the Richard B. Russell National School Lunch Act (1946), specified a federal school meal program for students from low-income families. This program grants cash reimbursements to schools across the country for meals served to eligible students. The School Milk Program (1954) authorized milk reimbursements to schools for students with similar qualifications.

The Child Nutrition Act (1966) formalized the School Breakfast Program. The Healthy, Hunger-Free Kids Act (2010), as part of the Child Nutrition Act reauthorization, sanctioned reimbursements to schools for Child and Adult Care Food (e.g., After-School Snack and Fresh Fruit and Vegetable Program). The Healthy, Hunger-Free Kids Act intended to improve students' eating habits by increasing the consumption of fruits, vegetables, and grains, while minimizing children eating foods with sugar, sodium, and high calories (Wood, Thompson, & Crampton, 2019).

The Improving Child Nutrition Integrity and Education Act (2016) reformed federal child nutrition policies to allow states and schools more flexibility in implementation. The reauthorization mandated the U.S. Department of Agriculture to review and update federal meal patterns and nutrition standards every 3 years (Congressional Research Service, 2019a).

The U.S. Department of Agriculture administers the national school meal programs through the Food and Nutrition Service and distributes funds to states for meals served to eligible LEA children. The SEA retains responsibility for oversight and administration of the federal school meal programs, including monitoring operations and distributing federal flow-through reimbursements as well as authorized commodities (U.S. Department of Agriculture, 2019a).

Custodial application and direct certification by the Supplemental Nutrition Assistance Program or Temporary Assistance for Needy Families agencies govern student eligibility in school meal programs. To validate eligibility, most LEAs accept household applications with self-declared income and household sizes. School employees compare this data with the annually adjusted income thresholds based on the Consumer Price Index for student eligibility in the program (U.S. Department of Agriculture, 2019a).

Children from families with incomes at or below 130 percent of the national poverty level may receive free meals. Children from families between 130 and 185 percent of the national poverty level qualify for reduced-price meals by application. Children from families with incomes over 185 percent of the national poverty level pay the school's full price for meals (U.S. Department of Agriculture, 2019a).

To obtain federal reimbursement, school personnel must accurately count, record, and claim the number of reimbursable meals served to students by category (e.g., free, reduced-price, or full price). A school staff member submits meal counts to district personnel. With proper student eligibility documentation on file, the staff records the number of reimbursable district meals and presents the sum to the state department of education via computer programs. The state's child nutrition office at the department of education holds responsibility to reimburse the district for allowable meals upon receipt of funds from the U.S. Department of Agriculture (Congressional Research Service, 2019a; Illinois State Board of Education, 2019).

A breakfast program grants additional reimbursement to schools that serve at least 40 percent or more school lunches to children who qualify for free or reduced-price meals (U.S. Department of Agriculture, 2019c).

The Special Milk Program now offers milk to children in schools that do not participate in other school meal programs. When a school participates in the National School Lunch or School Breakfast Program, children enrolled in half-day prekindergarten to grade 12 may not access the program (U.S. Department of Agriculture, 2019b).

Schools with high percentages of students from low-income families can offer meals at no charge to all students in a district through the Community Eligibility Provision. This provision encourages meal program participation, helps schools reduce labor costs, and fosters federal revenues. Because families do not complete applications and schools do not certify individual students, the process reduces the paperwork for schools and families along with streamlining district payments. School staff members simply count served meals and confirm that each student consumed a lunch and/or breakfast per day (Congressional Research Service, 2019a; Maurice, Russo, FitzSimmons, & Furtado, 2019).

For the monthly school meal program cash reimbursement, an LEA must have an efficient, effective accounting system to process receipts and expenditures. Sound accounting principles account for financial data collection in a timely, reliable, and consistent manner with the incorporation of internal control systems to minimize the risk of misusing funds. Chapter 5 details information on school accounting.

The monthly SEA and LEA school meal programs' reimbursement totals all eligible meals, breakfasts, and milk served by category. To review the annual notification on the *Federal Registrar* for the National School Lunch, Breakfast, and School Milk programs, click or search for https://www

.federalregister.gov/documents/2018/07/19/2018-15465/national-school
-lunch-special-milk-and-school-breakfast-programs-national-average-payments
maximum.

## Career and Technical Education Program

The Carl D. Perkins Career and Technical Education Act (2006), reauthorized with the Strengthening Career and Technical Education for the 21st Century Act (2018), also referred to as Perkins V, delivers formula grants to states for progressing career and technical education at secondary and postsecondary schools. Over 90 percent of the funds appropriated under the Perkins grant allocates Basic Grants (Association for Career and Technical Education, 2018).

Allowable expenditures for career and technical programs permit substitute personnel salaries and benefits, marketing and promotional materials, equipment, and instructional supplies to acquire students' occupational skills. Up to 5 percent of grant funding may be expended for program administration (Association for Career and Technical Education, 2018). To examine the SEA allocation formula for Perkins IV, which remained the same as Perkins V, click or search for https://www.everycrsreport.com/reports/R44542 .html#_Toc454531825.

## E-Rate Program

Based on the Telecommunications Act (1996), the Federal Communications Commission created the E-Rate program for schools and libraries to access affordable telecommunications services. This program specifies 20 to 90 percent discounts on telecommunications services, internet access, internal connections, and basic maintenance. The E-Rate program assures the most affluent school districts at least a 20 percent discount; otherwise, the percentage of district students eligible for the National School Lunch Program dictates the discount level. The Universal Service Administrative Company, an independent, not-for-profit corporation, administers the E-Rate program on behalf of the Federal Communications Commission. Every phone bill in the United States automatically imposes a Universal Service Fee to finance the program (Universal Service Administrative Company, 2019).

Although each school in the nation is eligible for E-Rate discounts, schools must apply for E-Rate funding; the state department of education often guides the application process. When approved, schools typically garner discounts through lower telecommunication costs by notification on the school's monthly telephone or internet service bills. The Universal Service Administration Company employees authorize the discounted percentage based on the school community's wealth and distribute monies to the service providers (Universal Service Administrative Company, 2019).

A school district staff may verify the discount scale for category 1 and 2 services with the percentage discount for urban and rural districts as well as the percentage of LEA students eligible for the National School Lunch Program. In category 1, telecommunication services include data transmission, internet access, and voice. Category 2 involves broadband and basic internal internet connections along with maintenance (Universal Service Administration Company, 2019). To check the E-Rate discount scale, click or search for https://www.erateadvantage.com/e-rate-discount-matrix.

## School-Based Medicaid Program

In accord with the Social Security Amendments (1965), U.S. Congress annually appropriates funds to match a state's cost of medical assistance for students from low-income families. The U.S. Department of Health and Human Services authorizes the Centers for Medicare and Medicaid Services to distribute Medicaid funds to states. The state retains a share based on the average per-person income in the state in comparison with the average per-person income in the United States (Medicaid and CHIP Payment and Access Commission, 2018).

The Medicare Catastrophic Coverage Act (1988) permits payments to schools for billable, medically necessary services mandated on a child's individualized education program. The federal requirements for the Medicaid program apply in all states, although the federal and state governments jointly administer Medicaid. Each state, therefore, establishes unique rules in affiliation with the federal guidelines (Alexander & Alexander, 2019; Medicaid and CHIP Payment and Access Commission, 2018).

When states permit districts to access federal funds under Medicaid for school-based health and related services commanded by the Individuals with Disabilities Education Act (IDEA), the state establishes a reimbursement system in which districts accept payments during the year from the state Medicaid agency. Each state establishes the Medicaid reimbursement rate for each reimbursable service supplied by the LEA. Districts must comply with specific Medicaid requirements regarding service documentation and claims submission (Medicaid and CHIP Payment and Access Commission, 2018).

Covered services may include, but are not limited to, physical, occupational, speech, and audiology therapy services; psychological counseling; nursing; and eligible transportation services. While most states fund evaluations, individual screenings, and administrative services, fewer states authorize group screening or treatment reimbursements. Many school districts contract with private firms to process district Medicaid claims (Medicaid and CHIP Payment and Access Commission, 2018).

Medicaid spending on school-based and related Medicaid administrative services was estimated to be $4.5 billion in fiscal year 2017. Although most states permit school-based Medicaid billing, less than 50 percent of Oregon districts sought Medicaid reimbursement. Due to Medicaid's complex administrative and paperwork requirements, small and rural districts were the least likely to participate. In Michigan, on the other hand, 100 percent of the districts participated in the program (AASA, The School Superintendents Association, 2019b).

To grow district participation in the school-based Medicaid program, education and health care advocates should work with leaders in the federal government to pass legislation that will streamline the process and reduce administrative burdens on districts. By reducing overhead costs and adding resources, school districts will more readily participate in the school-based Medicaid program (AASA, The School Superintendents Association, 2019b).

State information for the school-based Medicaid program may be available on a state department of education, government, or Medicaid website. To ask questions about a state's school-based Medicaid program, click or search for https://www.medicaid.gov/about-us/contact-us/contact-state-page.html and select a state.

## COMPETITIVE GRANTS

U.S. Congress authorizes competitive grants by annual congressional budget allocations. The federal government annually distributed more than $100 billion through discretionary grants for all programs. SEAs, LEAs, for-profit organizations, private agencies, charter schools, consortiums, and higher education institutes may apply for discretionary grants. The U.S. Department of Education devises program regulations that describe the procedures to administer an education grant and the criteria to evaluate an application (U.S. Department of Education, 2019a).

The U.S. Department of Education (2019a) lists all congressional grant competitions executed by the department. These discretionary grants target specific initiatives, such as educational research, school improvement, or charter school advancement. Individual awards range from $40,000 to millions of dollars, and some awards continue for 5 years once approved. A few discretionary grants include the following:

- Education Innovation and Research Program supports evidence-based innovations designed to enhance student achievement in science, technology, engineering, and mathematics.
- Educational Technology, Media, and Materials for Individuals with Disabilities Program serves to further results for children with disabilities by promoting the development, demonstration, and use of technology.
- Expanding Opportunity through Quality Charter Schools Program authorizes state grants to augment the number of high-quality charter schools available to traditionally underserved students across the United States.

Grants.gov (https://www.grants.gov) is the central repository and clearinghouse for over 1,000 federal discretionary grant programs. The Grants.gov system institutes a centralized access point for federal agencies (e.g., U.S. Department of Education) to announce grants. This website poses an online presence for SEAs and LEAs to discover and apply for discretionary grants. Federal agencies validate the application receipt on the website. The Grants.gov website and its related YouTube channel deliver grant writing assistance, application instructions, and training videos.

To apply for a federal discretionary grant, an applicant obtains a packet from the U.S. Department of Education or Grants.gov website. The application notice includes applicable statutes, program regulations, instructions, evaluation criteria, and related forms. The applicant must meticulously follow the transmittal instructions, thoroughly complete the application by the deadline, and electronically submit the finalized application on the website (Grants.gov, n.d.).

Upon submission, a federal department of education staff member screens the application for eligibility and thoroughness. When an application does not meet the program eligibility conditions, a staff member notifies the applicant and informs them that the application is not in consideration for funding nor subject to review. When an application meets the requirements, the reviewers score the application contents against the selection standards. When department staff members decide not to fund a request, they notify the contact person and explain the reasons for not funding the proposed application (Grants.gov, n.d.).

When an application is fundable, a department staff representative informs the contact person as well as the grantee's congressional district members about the award. After postaward conferences, the CFO/treasurer sets up an account and deposits the funds into the specific account. Other grantee obligations during the grant period involve performing and documenting the work as described in the approved application, communicating regularly with the department's program staff, and reporting all required information to the department, including a final expenditure or performance report (Grants.gov, n.d.).

## FUNDING FOR NONPUBLIC AND
## PUBLIC CHARTER SCHOOLS

### Nonpublic Schools

Title I, Parts A and C; Title II, Part A; Title III, Part A; Title IV, Parts A and B; and Title VI, Part B programs under the Elementary and Secondary Education Act mandated equitable services for nonpublic schools, students, and staff members. The LEA must apportion a share of Title I, Part A funds for services to eligible nonpublic schools. To ascertain the Title I allocation for an eligible nonpublic school, an LEA representative in the nonpublic school's attendance area verifies both the number of children aged 5 to 17 in low-income families attending the public school and the number of characteristically alike children enrolled in the nonpublic school (Izard, 2019).

An LEA staff member then calculates the proportional ratio of children from low-income families who attend the nonpublic school compared with those identical children in the public school. To establish the funding portion for nonpublic school Title I services, the LEA staff member multiplies the proportional ratio by the LEA's total Title I, Part A allocation (Izard, 2019).

For LEAs receiving authorized Title I, Part C monies, the LEA must grant equitable services for migrant nonpublic school students aged 3 to 21 to address needs in accordance with the law. The LEA staff, however, may choose when the number of eligible nonpublic school students is too few to serve. The LEA staff may adopt cost-effective methods to serve small numbers of nonpublic migrant students. The nonpublic school representative retains the opportunity to opt out of services after the mandated consultation with the LEA staff, For Title I, Parts A and C, an LEA representative must consult with nonpublic school personnel regarding the funds (Izard, 2019).

Title II, Part A regulations permit a nonpublic school to accept a share of the LEA's Title II, Part A allocation minus administrative costs. The Title II, Part B requirements dictate that equitable services under this program be available for nonpublic schoolteachers who teach in eligible school districts with awarded grants. To calculate the Title II, Parts A and B LEA per-pupil ratio, an LEA staff member divides the allocation, after administrative costs, by the LEA student enrollment (Izard, 2019).

To compute the nonpublic school Title II, Part A funding for bolstering educator quality and student success and Title II, Part B funding for mathematics and science partnerships, an LEA staffer multiplies the LEA per-pupil share by the number of enrolled nonpublic school students served within the LEA. For Title II, Parts A and B, an LEA representative must consult with nonpublic school personnel regarding the funds. The nonpublic school staff retains the opportunity to opt out of a project after the given consultation (Izard, 2019).

For nonpublic school Title III, Part A funding, an LEA employee computes the proportional ratio of the number of English language learners and immigrant children served by the nonpublic school in comparison with the number of representatively similar children served by the LEA. To calculate the nonpublic school's share of Title IV, Part A funds, the LEA agent, by formula, multiplies the proportional ratio by the LEA allocation. Nonpublic schools may compete for Title IV, Part B funding to expand activities in community learning centers (Izard, 2019).

Nonpublic schools are ineligible to participate in the Title V, Part B—Rural Education Achievement Program and the Title VI, Part A, Subpart 1—Indian Education Formula Grants (Council for American Private Education, 2016). The McKinney-Vento Act does not apply to privately funded schools; therefore, nonpublic schools remain removed from educating or transporting homeless children. Public schools, however, should offer Title VII, Subtitle B services to students experiencing homelessness who attend nonpublic schools (Schoolhouse Connection, 2019).

Under the Individuals with Disabilities Education Act (IDEA), LEAs must expend a proportionate share of IDEA Part B, Sections 611 and 619 to ensure special education and related services for nonpublic schoolchildren with special needs. To compute the IDEA allocation for an eligible nonpublic school, an LEA representative verifies both the number of children with special needs who attend the public school and the number of children with special needs attending the nonpublic school (Congressional Research Service, 2019d).

An LEA agent then compares the number of children with special needs who attend the nonpublic school with the eligible students in the public school to figure the proportional ratio. To calculate the nonpublic school IDEA special education funding, by formula, an LEA representative multiplies the proportional ratio (i.e., percentage) by the LEA's total IDEA allocation (Congressional Research Service, 2019d).

The National School Lunch Program and other federally assisted meal programs function at nonpublic schools in the same manner as public schools. Nonpublic schools must follow the same student eligibility regulations as public schools, and meals must meet federal expectations. Nonpublic schools that choose to participate in the lunch and other meal programs accept the same reimbursements as public schools (U.S. Department of Agriculture, 2019a).

Nonpublic schools that deliver career and technical education, particularly high schools, are eligible to collect Perkins funding in the same manner as public schools that offer such training (Association for Career and Technical Education, 2018). The E-Rate program affords the same discounts to nonpublic schools as public schools (Universal Service Administrative Company, 2019).

## Public Charter Schools

Charter schools are also eligible for federal funding. The Elementary and Secondary Education Act does not offer any statutory or regulatory language that directly addresses how SEAs should grant Title funding to charter schools; however, state charter laws may lend guidance. Public charter schools classified by state law as independent LEAs qualify for Title funding in the same manner as traditional public LEAs (U.S. Department of Education, 2019c).

In charter schools recognized as part of the LEA by state law, the allotted federal dollars vary greatly by state and depend on arrangements between the charter school and resident district. For this type of charter school, the district retains responsibility for the charter school's student services (U.S. Department of Education, 2019c). Figure 4.1 illustrates the flow of federal entitlement dollars based on a charter school's legal status.

Federal laws dictate eligibility requirements, administrative regulations, allocations, and the use of Title and IDEA funds. A state's charter school law may stipulate regulations regarding the retrieval of Title and IDEA program funds from the SEA. Eighteen states and the District of Columbia do not specify any relevant statute related to charter schools' access to Title funding, and 31 states and the District of Columbia do not direct charter schools in retrieving IDEA, Part B funds (Ziebarth, 2019).

Nine states offer limited guidance to obtain Title dollars, and six states issue limited information to access IDEA, Part B funds. States with limited statutory language indicate that charter schools may obtain federal grants as stated in law, but the laws generally fail to indicate the process to apply for funding (Ziebarth, 2019).

Seventeen states offer detailed guidance to obtain Title dollars, and seven states detail information to access IDEA, Part B funds. For states with comprehensive guidance to access federal funding, the charter school law explains the procedures to retrieve the federal monies, when they choose to participate in the federal program (Ziebarth, 2019). To see state-by-state legal standing for accessing federal categorical funding, click or search for the

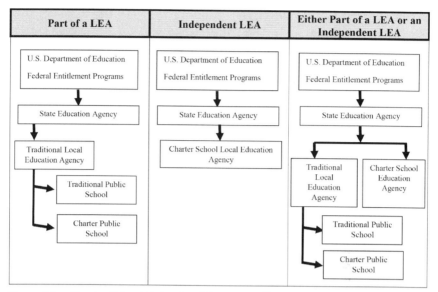

**Figure 4.1. Charter School Federal Entitlement Funding Stream**
*Source:* Author created.

National Alliance for Public Charter Schools website at https://www.public charters.org/our-work/charter-law-database.

Charter schools may participate in the national school meal programs (Food Research & Action Center, 2019). Charter schools, operating like LEAs, retain eligibility for Perkins funding (Association for Career and Technical Education, 2018). The Universal Service Administrative Company (2019) stated charter schools with LEA status may collect E-Rate funding at the same discount rates as traditional LEAs.

The discretionary Title IV, Part C—Expanding Opportunities through Quality Charter Schools grant offers state funding to open new charter schools and replicate high-performing charter schools. The discretionary Title V, Part B, Subpart 1—State Charter School Facilities Incentive Program grant matches federal funds with nonfederal dollars to support financing charter school facilities (Office of Innovation and Improvement, 2019b).

## PRIVATE FUNDING SOURCES

When schools face mounting fiscal demands and diminishing resources, public and nonpublic schools often rely on corporations, foundations, and individual donations to supplement funding. Private foundations are nonprofit institutes established to help fund charitable organizations, including schools. Nationwide, philanthropic giving through foundations and corporations averaged less than 1 percent of a typical school budget (Learning Landscape, 2016). Foundations and corporations offer funding through regulations; whereas, legislative bodies institute governmental entitlement and discretionary grants via statutes.

Seeking grant dollars may be a time-consuming, frustrating process whether originating from an entitlement, governmental discretionary, or private funding. Successfully writing a grant involves several steps: planning and searching sources, writing and submitting the proposal to the grantmaker, and completing follow-up activities after the award or rejection (O'Neal-McElrath, Kanter, & English, 2019).

## Step 1—Planning and Searching

For the successful grant seeker, grant writing begins by planning the project and searching for potential funding sources. Before spending too much time on the proposal, the grant searcher should discuss the project idea with supervisors and request authorization to proceed. When supervisors do not offer approval to proceed, the grant seeker should avoid wasting staff time and eliminate conflicts with other funding possibilities by abandoning the project idea. With prior approval, the grant seeker should clarify the project's purpose, define broad goals, and weigh funding needs in consultation with supervisors (O'Neal-McElrath et al., 2019).

Upon agreement to proceed, the grant pursuer should search for funding sources, evaluate needs in alignment with potential grant opportunities, and gather requests for proposal guidelines. When searching for potential private or governmental grants, the grant seeker should analyze each grant's specific instructions, such as

- grantmaker's purpose for funding,
- school or district eligibility,
- award levels,
- proposal format and timeframe,
- submission requirements, and
- evaluation processes.

To search for grants, the Foundation Center (https://candid.org/?fcref=lr) maintains comprehensive databases to locate foundation funding and offers training materials to assist in writing foundation, corporate, and individual donation grants. The Council on Foundations' locator (https://www.cof.org/

community-foundation-locator) qualifies accredited community foundations by state. The School Funding Center (http://www.schoolfundingcenter.info/index.aspx), a pay-per-subscription service, claims to retain every grant available to schools in a specific state database.

## Step 2—Writing and Submitting the Proposal

When a grant's instructions require a team to complete the application, technical writers, program experts, and interested parties should assist with the project. Grant developers must gather relevant supporting materials (e.g., facts, statistics, and testimony) and analyze a grant application's substance. The proposal guidelines normally offer thorough instructions about the grant's submission. Some grantmakers are very strict, and evaluators may not consider an application that misses an element like an authorized signature. Particular specifications may contain the number of copies, length of allowable pages, and submission format (O'Neal-McElrath et al., 2019).

When writing the proposal, following the grantmaker's instructions and meeting timelines stand critical. When the applicant does not flawlessly follow the directions nor timelines, the grant reviewer may view the proposal as carelessly written and elect not to read past the inaccuracies regardless of the application's plan. Proposal sections often enclose a brief narrative or summary, organization data, needs statement, project description, budget page, and appendices with support material (O'Neal-McElrath et al., 2019).

The summary is a vital section because reviewers may elect to read the entire proposal only after looking at the concluding narrative. O'Neal-McElrath et al. (2019) suggested composing the summary after writing the proposal to highlight key points (i.e., grantmaker's interests, goals, and enthusiasm for the project). With electronic submissions, grantmakers typically limit responses by restricting the word count for a permissible answer.

The needs description clarifies the reasons funding is necessary. Convincing the reviewer that the need is genuine with relevant, documented evidence stands crucial. Connecting the local need with a widely shared issue that matches the grantmaker's interest reinforces the chance of success (Geever, 2017; O'Neal-McElrath et al., 2019).

The project description may incorporate subsections, such as goals, objectives, staffing, methods, and evaluations. Project goals substantiate what the overall proposal will accomplish. Concrete, realistic, measurable, and achievable objectives in a well-defined timeframe support the proposal's steps to accomplish the goals. The proposal's methods describe the precise activities to achieve the objectives. The activity section also presents the order and timing of tasks (Geever, 2017; O'Neal-McElrath et al., 2019).

Well-thought, precisely written strategies assist the reviewer to visualize the project's enactment. Tapping competent, key project personnel to implement the proposal's activities with defined roles and discernible qualifications strengthens the proposal. The evaluation portion describes the manner in which assessments will be collected, explains the project's analysis, and reports project results. Supportive qualitative and quantitative data augments the project's success in meeting the proposal's goals and objectives; thus, evaluations should closely link with the targets (Geever, 2017; O'Neal-McElrath et al., 2019).

The proposal's budget may be as simple as a one-page statement or a more complex financial justification. The budget usually itemizes projected expenses to execute the proposal matched against the supplied revenue. In-kind contributions may be necessary. In preparing a budget page, the applicant should review the proposed narrative and consider allowable expenses found in the application guidelines. Permissible costs may be in three categories: personnel, direct, and administrative (Geever, 2017; O'Neal-McElrath et al., 2019).

Personnel expenses comprise salary, benefits, and related costs for those individuals who will fulfill the project. Direct expenses are nonpersonnel expenses and may contain items such as supplies, equipment, or materials. Administrative costs typically specify administrative salaries, benefits, or nonsalary operational expenses incurred to support a project. Many grants do not allow administrative expenses (Geever, 2017; O'Neal-McElrath et al., 2019). The budget request, above all, should be realistic to accomplish the project successfully and justify the project's goals. The zero-based budgeting methodology, as discussed in chapter 5, a constructive process to develop a grant budget.

Grantmakers may request a variety of supplemental materials often arranged in the appendices. O'Neal-McElrath et al. (2019) reported the grantor may request a copy of the school's tax-exempt status, personnel list, support letters, or a current financial statement. After verifying all the obligatory application elements, the proposal is ready for submission.

## Step 3—Completing Follow-up Activities

Submitting the proposal, however, does not conclude the grant process. Review procedures vary widely, and grant reviewers may examine a proposal for weeks or months before making a decision. During the review process, the grantmaker may ask for supplementary information. When a grantor does not fund a proposal, the applicant should carefully scrutinize the reviewer's comments, including strengths and weaknesses when offered. A grantor may fund a thoughtfully revised, resubmitted proposal in future funding rounds.

In the meantime, the applicant should continue to look for other financial avenues and stay encouraged (Geever, 2017; O'Neal-McElrath et al., 2019).

When a grantor funds a proposal, the grantee should fulfill the proposal as written and appropriately utilize the awarded dollars. Clarifying responsibilities at the project's onset, particularly with respect to financial reporting, prevents misunderstandings and future problems (Geever, 2017; O'Neal-McElrath et al., 2019).

After a grant award, a district business office staff member immediately arranges accounts to accept the monies. Chapter 5 will explain accounting details. Throughout implementation, the grantmaker may request updates on the project's progress. Situations may arise that necessitate proposal or budgetary changes to accomplish the project's goals. The grantee should precisely follow the grantmaker's guidelines when considering changes. To conclude a project, the grantor may demand a final expenditure report.

## SUMMARY

Education is primarily a function delegated to the states by the Tenth Amendment to the U.S. Constitution. Although federal and private revenue for a school district operation is meager in comparison to state and local funding, these monetary resources remain vital for school functions.

Every Student Succeeds Act and other federally authorized legislation approved various entitlement programs, with specific funding levels established through the annual budgetary process. A prescriptive formula for each entitlement program authorizes SEA and LEA allocations.

LEAs generally obtain entitlement monies from the SEA through similar formulas as prescribed in the federal statues for state allocations. Title I, Part A remains the largest federal entitlement program, although the government annually authorizes billions of dollars through other entitlement grants.

Congress also sanctions various discretionary (i.e., competitive) grants in which the SEA or LEA, or both, personnel may choose to participate. To apply for a discretionary federal grant, an applicant must closely comply with the U.S. Department of Education timeline and instructions.

Foundations, corporations, and individual donations offer private funding for schools using a similar application design as many governmental formula and discretionary grants. Although these private funds have minimal impact on a school budget, successful grant writing commands much planning, thorough researching, clear writing, timely submission, and meticulous follow-up action.

Discretionary federal dollars and private funds for public, nonpublic, and charter schools hold opportunities to assist in educating students. To access these funds, laws and regulations describe the process by which public, non-public, and charter schools must follow to obtain monies, when they choose to participate.

## PROJECTS

1. Identify and report, by program, the federal entitlement revenues that your school receives.
2. Identify and report, by program, the federal competitive revenues that your school collects.
3. Explore your jurisdiction's department of education website and report the guidelines for the delivery of federal programs.
4. Investigate and explain, by formula, at least one state education agency and one local education agency's Title allocation.
5. Research and bookmark the following websites for future reference to federal and private grants:
   - Grants.gov (https://www.grants.gov),
   - Foundation Center (https://candid.org/?fcref=lr),
   - Council on Foundations' locator (https://www.cof.org/community -foundation-locator), and
   - School Funding Center (http://www.schoolfundingcenter.info/index.aspx).
6. Determine a financial need in your school, collaborate with a supervisor about pursuing a grant, identify grant sources, acquire proposal guidelines, write a proposal, and submit the application to the grantmaker for review.
7. Identify, by program, the federal funding for a nonpublic or charter school.

*Chapter Five*

# Accounting Services

**OBJECTIVES**

After reading this chapter, you should be able to

✓ explain and interpret the school fund accounting system (NELP 5.3, 6.1, 6.2, 6.3);
✓ distinguish between the various budget processes and create a budget (NELP 5.3, 6.1, 6.2, 6.3);
✓ understand the rationale and processes for forecasts and audits (NELP 6.1, 6.2, 6.3); and
✓ differentiate between the budget and appropriation (NELP 5.3, 6.1, 6.2, 6.3).

During American education's earliest years, financial records were not intricate because one-room schools had a small number of students with relatively few financial transactions. During the twentieth century, however, student enrollments grew, states levied sales and income tax to pay for public education, and districts collected property tax.

With state taxes, funding for public schools increased, and basic aid formulas developed, commanding sophisticated standardized financial recordkeeping and reporting. Over time, bookkeeping advanced into accounting, the practice of recording, classifying, summarizing, reporting, and interpreting an organization's fiscal activities.

Fund accounting, forecasting, budgeting, appropriating, and auditing classify functions that complement the district's educational program. While designated school personnel separately conduct each task, duties closely intertwine and entail comprehensive computerized information systems (Brimley et al., 2020).

Nowadays, institutions of any size, public and nonpublic, cannot operate effectively without precise accounting services to process financial transactions. According to Schilling and Tomal (2019), school accounting departments

- receive and assign local, state, and federal revenue into proper fund accounts;
- prepare the budget, forecast finances, and appropriate monies;
- generate local, state, and federal reports;
- convey and publicize the district's financial position to the public, school board, staff, and governmental authorities;
- maintain fiscal accountability to ensure precise handling of money and safeguard against stolen, lost, or misused assets;
- approve expenditures through formal purchasing procedures;
- record, monitor, and pay obligations;
- establish business relationships with agencies and institutions, such as state and federal education departments, banks, insurance companies, retirement systems, and vendors; and
- conduct cost analyses to assess expenditures in light of educational achievements.

Citizens demand that school districts maintain an effectual fiscal management system. School officials substantiate fiscal accountability through judicious and transparent administration of the public's money. School accountability, these days, emphasizes student academic achievement in relationship to the costs of a suitable education. Because technological databases now detail student and staff demographics, academic achievements, and district budgets and appropriations, the availability of these statistics amplify public access on district websites, interest in school business, and scrutiny of data.

Although most school administrators have limited training in accounting, they should exhibit general knowledge, practice sound business principles, and possess competency regarding processes to ensure legal compliance, guarantee operation efficacy, safeguard assets, and acknowledge accurate recordkeeping. The CFO/treasurer and personnel in the business office must exhibit a keen awareness of accounting processes.

## FUND ACCOUNTING

To execute accounting services, districts employ fund accounting, a system of managing the flow of revenue receipts and expenditures. Fund accounting displays distinct fiscal accounts for recording, tracking, and reporting revenue along with documenting expenditures on financial reports (Schilling & Tomal, 2019).

Because school administrators and board of education members rely on fund accounting data to support daily operations, decision making, and performance, they must possess a basic understanding of the fund accounting system. CFO/treasurers, on the other hand, must exhibit a deeper understanding of fund accounting than school administrators.

Revenue and expenditure transactions dictate a standard structure with a combination of multidimensional codes. Although each jurisdiction maintains a unique codification structure (see table 5.1), the federal government guides states with a chart of accounts essential for federal reporting. The *Financial Accounting for Local and State School Systems* from the National Center for Education Statistics is the accounting authority for local and state governmental jurisdictions (Allison, 2015). Because the document information infrequently changes over the years, the U.S. Department of Education does not update the text very often.

All school districts track accounts with the federal/state codes in three main funds (e.g., government, proprietary, and fiduciary) accounts for national data collection (Schilling & Tomal, 2019).

- Government fund accounts, financed generally through taxes and intergovernmental revenue, include general, special revenue, debt service, and capital project funds. The general fund, the largest district operating account, retains unrestricted funds (e.g., property tax and state basic aid) and details expenditures for any legal purpose. General fund dollars may be commingled with other funds, as necessary, and reallocated in a future fiscal year when available. The special revenue fund receipts restricted funds from specific sources (e.g., categorical aid, federal entitlements, restricted tax levies, and athletic programs) and verifies payments for legal purposes. The capital project fund accounts for deposits from state building grants or permanent improvement levies. Expenditures in the capital project fund acquire equipment, construct and renovate buildings, or purchase land. The debt service fund accepts revenue from bond issues and records expenses on long-term debt obligations for principal, interest, and related costs. School personnel may not commingle special revenue, debt service, or capital project funds with other fund accounts (Schilling & Tomal, 2019).
- Proprietary fund accounts manage nongovernmental, business activities classified as either enterprise or internal service. The enterprise fund categorizes personnel, supplies, and service revenues from the bookstore, food service operation, and athletic program. The enterprise fund

also documents expenses in these endeavors. The internal service fund receipts income and expenses incurred from departments within the school district, such as central printing, duplicating, warehousing, or data processing (Schilling & Tomal, 2019).

- The fiduciary fund accounts maintain assets from endowments, donations, gifts, or partnerships with the district as the fund trustee. A district, for example, may have private-purpose trusts for pension accounts established for employee retirements or student scholarship funds. The school district staff oversees the fund and distributes the proceeds (i.e., principal and interest or interest only) in accord with the trust agreement. With fiduciary agency funds, the district holds assets in a custodial capacity for student clubs or governmental agencies. The student activity fund, for instance, receipts cash generated by student participation in an organization and expends monies to offset costs incurred by the group's activities. In a governmental agency fund, a small community library, for instance, may request a school district to receive the library property tax and administer expenses. Fiduciary funds may not support school operating costs (Schilling & Tomal, 2019).

After acknowledging the receipt of money, the CFO/treasurer assigns the revenue into a specific fund by purpose and source: local, state, or federal. Numerous accounts exist for local revenue (e.g., property tax and tuition) and unrestricted grants-in-aid (e.g., state basic aid). Other accounts may record restricted grants-in-aid revenue (e.g., state categorical programs and federal entitlements).

Per Allison (2015), the suggested federal revenue reporting dimensions with corresponding codes also involve the following:

- The receipt code acknowledges monies obtained by the district with a classification by source and type, such as levied taxes (1100), unrestricted grants-in-aid (3100), and federal restricted grants-in-aid (4500).
- The fund code distinguishes the purpose of receipts and the source: General Fund (01), Special Revenue Fund (02), Capital Projects (03), Debt Service (04), Enterprise Fund (05), Internal Revenue Fund (06), and Fiduciary Funds (07).
- The project dimension recognizes funding from restricted local, state, federal, and private sources.

The suggested receipt, fund, and project dimension codes classify revenue and expenditures; however, the federal government's detailed expenditure codes remain significantly more complex than the revenue codes.

Allison (2015) reported the following federal government's expenditure fields and codes:

- The program codes and elements classify the general activity designed to accomplish objectives in a specific program: regular elementary/secondary (100), special (200), and vocational (300).
- The function codes and components categorize a transaction's purpose: instruction (1000), pupil support services (2100), school administration (2300), operations and maintenance (2600), and student transportation (2700).
- The object codes and sections detail specific expenditures within a function: regular employee salaries (100), employee benefits for group health insurance (210), retirement (230), workers' compensation (260), purchased services (300), general supplies (600), and equipment (730).
- The project codes and segments describe expenditures by assignment: local (010–190), state (200–390), and federal (400–990).
- The instructional level codes and fields recognize expenses by grade level: elementary (10), middle (20), and secondary (30).

The field string explains every transaction in federal accounting terms, and each line captures a specific description regarding a transaction. Figure 5.1 illustrates the field sequence with corresponding codes from the broadest operational category (i.e., general fund) to the narrowest (i.e., instructional level). This line, thereby, describes a general fund transaction in the regular elementary/secondary program (100) for the instruction function (1000). The field string further details the expenditure by a regular employee salary (100) in a local project (010) at the elementary school (10).

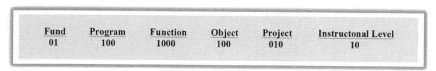

| Fund | Program | Function | Object | Project | Instructonal Level |
|------|---------|----------|--------|---------|--------------------|
| 01 | 100 | 1000 | 100 | 010 | 10 |

**Figure 5.1. Federal Codes with Expenditure Account Structure**
*Source:* Allison, G. S. (2015). *Financial accounting for local and state school systems: 2014 edition* (NCES 2015-347). Washington, DC: U.S. Department of Education, National Center for Education Statistics.

Although jurisdictions may report financial data to the federal government via federal codes, jurisdictions also maintain a uniform standardized account coding system for public school districts. The jurisdiction codes may not coincide with the federal chart of accounts. Astute school officials will be familiar with the unique chart of accounts for a jurisdiction. Table 5.1 displays a resource for each jurisdiction's account code manual.

**Table 5.1.  Account Code Manuals**

| Jurisdiction | State Account Codes |
| --- | --- |
| Alabama | https://www.alsde.edu/sec/leaaccount/Pages/acctman-all.aspx |
| Alaska | https://education.alaska.gov/publications/chart_of_accounts.pdf |
| Arizona | https://www.azauditor.gov/sites/default/files/USFRCOA21319.pdf |
| Arkansas | https://docplayer.net/11723268-State-of-arkansas-arkansas-financial-accounting-handbook.html |
| California | https://www.cde.ca.gov/fg/ac/sa/documents/csam2019complete.pdf |
| Colorado | https://www.cde.state.co.us/cdefinance/fpp_coa |
| Connecticut | http://www.osc.ct.gov/stateacct/sam/index.html |
| Delaware | http://budget.delaware.gov/accounting-manual/documents/chapter03.pdf |
| Florida | https://www.myfloridacfo.com/division/AA/COA/Redesign2014/ChartofAccountFinalReport-2014-01-15.pdf |
| Georgia | https://www.gadoe.org/Finance-and-Business-Operations/Financial-Review/Pages/LUAS-Manual.aspx |
| Hawaii | http://www.hawaiipublicschools.org/Standards%20of%20Practice/SP1000.pdf |
| Idaho | https://www.sde.idaho.gov/finance/files/financial-info/ifarms/Summary-of-Codes.doc |
| Illinois | https://www.isbe.net/Documents/ipam.pdf |
| Indiana | https://www.in.gov/sboa/files/sch2010toc.pdf |
| Iowa | https://educateiowa.gov/pk-12/school-business-and-finance/accounting-and-reporting/uniform-financial-accounting |
| Kansas | https://www.ksde.org/Portals/0/School%20Finance/guidelines_manuals/Accounting%20Handbook18.pdf |
| Kentucky | https://education.ky.gov/districts/FinRept/Pages/Fund%20Balances,%20Revenues%20and%20Expenditures,%20Chart%20of%20Accounts,%20Indirect%20Cost%20Rates%20and%20Key%20Financial%20Indicators.aspx |
| Louisiana | https://www.doa.la.gov/osrap/library/Publications/revisedandrereleasedppm/CHAP13.pdf |
| Maine | https://www1.maine.gov/audit/documents/2007mcoa.pdf |
| Maryland | http://archives.marylandpublicschools.org/NR/rdonlyres/14932C50-4E7C-41F7-9886-7673EBBA6A96/20518/FINANCIALREPORTINGMANUALREVISEDFINALMAY620092.pdf |
| Massachusetts | http://www.doe.mass.edu/finance/accounting/eoy/ |
| Michigan | https://www.michigan.gov/documents/appendix_33974_7.pdf |
| Minnesota | https://www.leg.state.mn.us/docs/2018/other/181048.pdf |
| Mississippi | https://www.mdek12.org/OSF/AccountingManual |
| Missouri | https://dese.mo.gov/sites/default/files/sf-CompleteFinancialAccountingManual-July2018.pdf |
| Montana | https://opi.mt.gov/LinkClick.aspx?fileticket=XxBq3DErztc%3D&portalid=182 |
| Nebraska | https://www.nebraska.gov/rules-and-regs/regsearch/Rules/Education_Dept_of/Title-92/Chapter-02.pdf |

| Jurisdiction | State Account Codes |
| --- | --- |
| Nevada | http://budget.nv.gov/uploadedFiles/budgetnvgov/content/IAudits/Forms/Acctg_PoliciesProcedures.pdf |
| New Hampshire | https://www.education.nh.gov/data/documents/fin_acct_handbk.pdf |
| New Jersey | http://www.state.nj.us/education/finance/fp/af/coa/coa1718.pdf |
| New Mexico | https://webnew.ped.state.nm.us/wp-content/uploads/2018/01/SHSB_3.Supplement_ver_4.0_March_2016.pdf |
| New York | https://www.osc.state.ny.us/localgov/pubs/arm_schools.pdf |
| North Carolina | https://www.dpi.nc.gov/districts-schools/district-operations/financial-and-business-services/school-district-finance-operations/chart-accounts www.dpi.state.nc.us/docs/fbs/finance/reporting/coa/2005-06manual.pdf |
| North Dakota | https://www.nd.gov/dpi/sites/www/files/documents/SFO/NDSFARM%202018%20(2).pdf |
| Ohio | https://ohioauditor.gov/publications/uniform_school_accounting_system_user_manual.pdf |
| Oklahoma | https://sde.ok.gov/financial-accounting |
| Oregon | https://www.oregon.gov/ode/students-and-family/childnutrition/SNP/Documents/2012-pbam-manual.pdf |
| Pennsylvania | https://www.education.pa.gov/Documents/Teachers-Administrators/School%20Finances/Comptrollers%20Office/Manual%20of%20Accounting.pdf |
| Rhode Island | https://www.ride.ri.gov/InformationAccountability/RIEducationData/UniformChartofAccounts.aspx |
| South Dakota | https://legislativeaudit.sd.gov/resources/schools/accountingmanual/School_Section_2/School_Section%202_Revenues-listing%20and%20definitions.pdf |
| Tennessee | https://comptroller.tn.gov/office-functions/la/resources/chart-of-accounts.html |
| Texas | https://tea.texas.gov/Finance_and_Grants/Financial_Accountability/Financial_Accountability_System Resource_Guide |
| Utah | https://www.schools.utah.gov/financialoperations/reporting?mid=2159&tid=3 |
| Vermont | https://education.vermont.gov/vermont-schools/school-finance/ucoa |
| Virginia | http://www.apa.virginia.gov/data/download/local_government/mauals/Uniform%20Financial%20Reporting%20Manual.docx |
| Washington | https://www.k12.wa.us/sites/default/files/public/safs/ins/acc/1819/sdam1819complete.pdf |
| Washington, DC | https://dcps.dc.gov/page/budget-and-finance |
| West Virginia | https://wvde.state.wv.us/finance/manuals/charts.pdf |
| Wisconsin | https://dpi.wi.gov/sfs/finances/wufar/overview |
| Wyoming | https://edu.wyoming.gov/downloads/schools/school-district-accounting-manual.pdf |

The following delineations, classified by state codes, distinguish expenditures based on Ohio's *Uniform School Accounting System* (Auditor of State, 2013), which is the most current version:

- The operational unit (OU) catalogs the specific attendance center where the activity occurs.
- The subject matter (SM) describes expenses by subject area.
- The special cost center (SCC) designates courses or bus routes.
- Job assignment (JA) tracks the expenditure to an employee's job classification.

Table 5.2 illustrates the account code string for an expenditure that originated from restricted revenue (e.g., Title I, Part A) and assigned to the Special Revenue Fund (572). This line-item appropriation distinguishes dollars for the instruction function (1270).

This line further signifies an object (11), a certified employee's salary and wage. The special cost center (SCC) dimension is a federal program activity (e.g., Title I) with 9060 assigned by the district. The Ohio Department of Education assigns the next code with the first two digits describing the subject area (SA) and the last four digits defining the subject (S). The 400000 code represents Title I.

The operational unit (OU) denotes the location of service (e.g., elementary school) with 006 assigned by the district. The instructional level (IL) codes the grade level. For the example (see table 5.2), expended services were coded 03, meaning this activity occurred in grade 3. The job assignment (JA) identifies the staff member's duties. The Ohio Department of Education creates and defines the 125 code. Table 5.2 shows the described financial activity with the account code string.

To record transactions, districts employ either a single-entry or double-entry accounting method. The single-entry accounting method assigns only one entry on the ledger for either a cash receipt or disbursement. The double-entry accounting method records debit expense entries for accounts and corresponding credit revenue entries to maintain a balance between assets and liabilities. A transaction's timing, considered the basis of accounting, stands critical in reporting revenue and expenditures. Three accounting methods log financial transactions: modified accrual, accrual, and cash. Each accounting format documents transactions and displays financial statements in a different format (Office of the New York State Comptroller, 2019).

The school's accounting department staff employs the modified accrual basis of accounting for general, special revenue, debt service, and capital project accounts (Office of the New York State Comptroller, 2019). The *Generally*

**Table 5.2. Ohio Expense Account Code String**

| Fund | Special Revenue Fund 572 |
|------|--------------------------|
| Function | Instruction 1270 |
| Object | Certified Salary 111 |
| SCC | Assigned 9060 |
| SA/S | DOE Number 400000 |
| OU | Elem. 001 |
| IL | Grade 03 |
| JA | Duty 125 |

*Source:* Auditor of State (2013).
*Note:* Codes illustrated in this table report the most current information from the Ohio *Uniform School Accounting System: User Manual.*

*Accepted Accounting Principles* (GAAP) uniform standards for reporting
financial statements as authorized by the Governmental Accounting Standards Board (GASB), command districts to account for transactions in the
general fund via the modified accrual basis. When accepting revenue using
the modified accrual basis, the designated employee records the money upon
direct receipt and documents expenditures when encumbered (i.e., obligated
by a purchase order). In this method, districts recognize revenues when they
become available and immediately acknowledge expenditures upon liability
(Schilling & Tomal, 2019).

To report and expend district enterprise and fiduciary accounts, the assigned employee utilizes the accrual basis to credit revenue when obligated,
as opposed to when directly received in the account. The district employee
records expenses when incurred. The cash basis acknowledges income upon
receipt by check or electronic deposit and documents expenditures when
paid. School districts do not use the cash basis method (Office of the New
York State Comptroller, 2019).

School officials communicate financial reports to local stakeholders
through internal documents. As stated by Schilling and Tomal (2019), a district's accounting department may generate the following internal documents:

- inventories to account for purchased equipment, particularly for audit sub-
  stantiation and insurance recovery;
- bank statements to reconcile end-of-the-month bank accounts;
- fund balance reports to show receipts, expenditures, and cash balances;
  and
- monthly budget/appropriation account summaries to detail cash receipts
  and disbursements.

The monthly budget/appropriation account summary is the most important report for building principals and supervisors to understand, read, and
interpret. To see an example of the monthly budget/appropriation account
summary, look at exhibit 7 in the appendices. This document captures the
following fiscal funds to date by account string (i.e., line):

- monthly revenues and expenditures,
- appropriated dollars,
- expendable cash,
- actual expenditures,
- current encumbrances, and
- unencumbered balances.

A district constructs financial records for outside governmental agencies via external reports, particularly through audits that monitor federal and state compliance regarding statutes and regulations. Both internal and external accounting documents verify the district's monetary status (Schilling & Tomal, 2019).

## FORECASTS

Many factors, including the status of the national economy, state fiscal health, and local dynamics (i.e., student enrollment and district initiatives), affect a district's fiscal position. Financial forecasting, a critical accounting function, describes the practice of predicting trends and changes on future district operations by examining actual historical data. Projecting student enrollments; predicting local, state, and federal revenues; envisioning expenditures; and anticipating costs associated with salary adjustments set baseline budgetary parameters and create the basis for assumptions to prepare budgets (Wood et al., 2019).

As per the Office of the New York State Comptroller (2019), multiyear fiscal forecasting

- analyzes trends, recognizes needs, and clarifies issues for budget preparation;
- facilitates strategic planning efforts with a fiscal impact analysis;
- enhances administrative decision making by revealing valuable insights into future inclinations;
- encourages dialogue between school officials and the community about long-range planning efforts; and
- ensures statutory and contractual fund balance compliance.

Student enrollment projections stand crucial for operational budgeting, staffing, and classroom distributions because school districts rely on student numbers to anticipate future needs and plan accordingly (Smith, 2017b).

When student enrollment dramatically increases, for instance, then increasing classroom spaces, adding bus routes, purchasing additional equipment and supplies, and expanding the staff may follow. To the contrary, when student enrollment declines and state aid establishes allocations on a per-pupil allotment, then a district may receive less state funding and may need to reduce future expenditures or seek a local initiative to bolster the budget.

Although various techniques forecast future student enrollment, the grade progression ratio method (i.e., cohort survival method) is a simple strategy to predict future student enrollment. With this tactic school officials first calculate the average progression of students from one grade to the next and then computes the effects of in- and out-migration patterns, including district housing trends and student transfers from homeschooling along with public, nonpublic, and charter schools (Smith, 2017b).

To estimate baseline data, the grade progression ratio method scrutinizes trends in kindergarten enrollment because the district's current kindergartners comprise tomorrow's students at upper grade levels through school system migration. Historical and projected area birth data assist in forecasting the number of kindergarten students intended to enroll. In addition to analyzing kindergarten enrollment, the grade progression ratio compares incoming kindergarten enrollment to outgoing grade 12 enrollment (Smith, 2017b).

By averaging the annual in- and out-migration student populations from homeschooling along with public, nonpublic, and charter schools by grade level, school officials form an assumption to project future student enrollment (Smith, 2017b). For instance, if the district lost 50 students, on average, to charter schools each year for the past 5 years, the assumption is the district will continue to lose 50 students in future years to charter schools unless other circumstances intervene.

To capture student in-migration, housing trends are another variable in the grade progression ratio method. The number of housing starts in any given year depends on a number of variables: interest rates, housing demand, developers' investments, and policymakers' decisions. For this variable, school officials multiply the number of unbuilt, approved residential units by the number of anticipated students per unit on average. This estimate provides school officials with the average number of students likely to enroll in the district in correlation with new housing units (Smith, 2017b).

When the number of housing starts in a district remains the same for several years, baseline data then assume that the in-migration of school-age children due to housing starts will remain the same as previous years. When the residential housing development for a district projects an increase, in-migration student numbers will rise. When school officials anticipate declining area population or the number of housing starts significantly decrease, in-migration for the school district may result in fewer students (Smith, 2017b).

School districts should annually project student enrollment, particularly in dynamic housing areas. San Francisco Unified School District school officials utilized a consultant to predict student enrollment because the city's housing development was very active (Lapkoff & Gobalet Demographic Research, Inc., 2018). Educational Data Systems and Education Logistics, Inc. offer popular computer software programs to predict student enrollment. Overall, five-year student projections remain more accurate than ten-year projections (Smith, 2017b).

As a compliance responsibility, Ohio is the only state in the Union that mandates school districts generate, maintain, and submit a general fund financial forecast to the state department of education. By contrast, 37 states and the District of Columbia do not acknowledge a forecast procedure; whereas, 12 states (e.g., California, Illinois, Indiana, Iowa, Michigan, Minnesota, Missouri, New York, Pennsylvania, Texas, Virginia, and Wisconsin) view district fiscal forecasting as a best practice.

The Ohio Department of Education (2019a) reported that forecasts (see appendix-exhibit 6) project revenue (e.g., general property tax, income tax, unrestricted grants-in-aid, restricted grants-in-aid, and total revenue), anticipate expenditures (e.g., personal services, employees' retirement and insurance benefits, purchased services, supplies and materials, capital outlay, and debt service), calculate beginning and ending cash balances, and determine outstanding encumbrances obliged by purchase orders.

The Michigan School Business Officials (2019) indicate that multiyear forecasting assists districts with the following indicators:

* revenue and expenditure data analyses,
* staffing and compensation commitments,
* medical plan tendencies,
* student enrollment projections,
* building renovation and classroom space requirements, and
* equipment and supply necessities.

To accomplish forecasting, computerized projection simulators allow districts to create multiple "what if" scenarios with spreadsheets, reports, charts, and graphs to predict varying outcomes based on district variables. Many districts across the country employ Forecast5 Analytics to conduct financial projections (Forecast5 Analytics, 2019; Illinois Statewide School Management Alliance, 2018). Dynamic Budget Projections, another projection alternative, partnered with Michigan schools to provide projections (Michigan School Business Officials, 2019). Large-scale database technology enables districts to compare complex budgetary scenarios.

## BUDGETS

A district's general fund operating budget anticipates revenues and estimates expenditures for a fiscal year. The budget, linked to financial accountability, serves as a blueprint for anticipated financial transactions and a means to inform the public about the district's operation. States with independent school districts mandate that the district staff prepares annual budgets because boards of education have a relatively free hand in deciding how, where, how much, and when to expend funds. Although personnel at dependent school districts also prepares and executes budgets, the parent government holds final approval (Wood et al., 2019).

Budget development is not the sole responsibility of one person; instead, the process is a team effort. The governing board in a few school districts designates the superintendent as the budget officer to develop the annual budget; however, the board of education in most districts usually tasks the CFO/treasurer or district business administrator (i.e., budget officer) to create the school budget (Wood et al., 2019).

While the budget officer remains statutorily responsible to prepare the final budget document, the budget officer works closely with the central office staff, principals, and department heads who propose financial data for their supervisory responsibilities. Employees may also offer input to supervisors (Wood et al., 2019).

Prior to final budget adoption, the budget officer prepares a preliminary budget and presents the document to the governing board. After adjustments, the budget officer finalizes the budget proposal before board approval. Many states mandate that the proposed final budget be available for public inspection prior to the adoption by the board (Office of the New York State Comptroller, 2019).

District residents in Connecticut, Maine, New Hampshire, New Jersey, and Vermont approve the school budget by referendum in conjunction with board of education authorization. Arizona school districts must hold elections to override a school district budget. To exceed the previous year's total program budget by more than 125 percent, Colorado school districts must pass a budget referendum (Ballotpedia, 2019). New York school district boards may authorize the electorate to vote on the budget (Office of the New York State Comptroller, 2019).

Although school districts across the country differ on the exact method for budget preparation, development usually consists of five sequential, interrelated activities (Wood et al., 2019):

- initiating the budget process,
- estimating revenue,
- envisioning the educational program,
- approximating expenditures, and
- balancing program needs against revenues and expenditures.

For Ohio school districts, the county budget commission (i.e., county treasurer, auditor and prosecuting attorney) certifies the available revenue before district personnel commences general fund budget development. A certificate of estimated resources (see appendix-exhibit 5) verifies unencumbered fund balances in the general fund, special revenue, debt service, capital projects, internal and fiduciary, and enterprise accounts (Ohio Department of Education, 2018).

The district's governing board approves the certificate and amendments prior to the July 1 temporary appropriation adoption and before the October 1 permanent appropriation approval (Ohio Department of Education, 2018). Table 5.3 shows a tentative budget calendar with a July 1 beginning date, which starts the fiscal year in 46 states.

**Table 5.3. Proposed Budget Calendar**

| Tentative Date | Action |
| --- | --- |
| December | Discuss budgetary process and calendar with governing board and staff. |
| January | Review five-year forecast. |
| January | Tabulate the General Fund Revenue Estimate (see table 5.4). |
| January | Receive Estimate of Resources for Ohio districts (see appendix-exhibit 5). |
| February | Collect data:<br>• Receive budget requests by Function and Object from supervisors and principals,<br>• Project student enrollment,<br>• Predict staffing,<br>• Resolve facility needs, and<br>• Review the negotiated agreement regarding class size limits, salary schedule changes, and employee benefit adjustments, when necessary.<br>Discuss the envisioned educational program and spending recommendations with staff and governing board. |
| March | Estimate General Fund Expenditures by Function and Object (see table 5.5). |
| April | Balance and file the preliminary budget proposal with a public notification. |
| May | Hold public hearing when necessary. |
| June | Revise the preliminary budget and appropriation measure. |
| June | Finalize the budget and appropriation measure. |
| Before July 1 | Approve the finalized budget (governing board or district resident vote). |
| Before July 1 | Adopt temporary appropriation measure after budget adoption. |
| After July 1 | Adopt permanent appropriation measure (governing board). |
| July–June | Recommend appropriation line transfers to governing board and implement as necessary. |

*Source:* Wood et al. (2019).

Over years, school districts across the country have employed various approaches to develop a budget. School districts generally enact the most workable budgeting method for their unique situation. Incremental line-item, zero-based, site-based, and performance-based budgeting remain the most popular tactics, although districts in reality rarely employ a single approach. Budgeting, most often, actually incorporates a combination of these budget strategies (Brimley et al., 2020).

The incremental line-item budgeting approach reviews the previous 2 years' operating budget accounts to generate budget data by fund, function, and object. For this budget method, the budget officer first examines actual revenue sources for each year and then allots an average percentage increase or decrease by source (Brimley et al., 2020).

With incremental line-item budgets, the budget officer compares the actual expenditures by line for the past 2 years because most expenditures continue year after year. The budget officer then adjusts each anticipated expenditure by the average increased or decreased percentage, depending on the trend. Incremental line-item budgeting is simple to understand and easy to prepare because of the straightforward application of average revenue and expense percentage trends. Critics, however, claim this model presents decision makers little useful data on program successes or failures (Brimley et al., 2020).

Zero-based budgeting does not guarantee financing expenditures from the previous year in the next fiscal cycle; therefore, this model is much different than incremental line-item budgeting. With zero-based budgeting, the budget officer begins with the known income. Each expenditure starts with a zero allocation (Brimley et al., 2020).

The budget officer must then justify the continuation of each expense, with a bottom-up prioritization process in accordance with the educational plan. This budgeting model becomes time-consuming and less appealing because of the complex decision making to defend each previous year's spending. Zero-based budgeting, however, is quite beneficial for program start-ups and advantageous to construct a grant application because of the confirmed income dollars and specified expenses to execute the grant (Brimley et al., 2020).

Site-based budgeting decentralizes the budgetary process by allocating resources to a particular site. This budgetary process bestows control to the people responsible for delivering the children's education. The scope of a realistic site-based budget is best limited to instructional supplies, materials, texts, and equipment; whereas, capital projects, debt repayment, transportation, insurance, and personnel costs should remain under the central office's authority (Brimley et al., 2020).

With the site-based approach, the school staff, on location, have greater input in decision making, more accountability, and fewer restrictions than other methods. However, the time and complexity to develop site-based budgets along with the on-site staff skills necessary to accomplish this budget type are often overwhelming (Smith, 2017b).

Performance-based or outcome-based budgeting, an offshoot of the Planning, Programming, Budgeting, and Evaluation System discussed in chapter 3, links resources to activities that best meet goals and measure outcomes. This methodology relies on a deliberate process regarding performance indicators and program targets as well as expenditure evaluations. With allocations linked to performance, unmet goals and objectives reflect modifications for the next fiscal cycle.

Evaluating programs and activities consumes vast amounts of staff time to acquire input and output indicators. In addition, some district functions (e.g., administration and auxiliary services) do not exact measurable student academic performance results. Considering the shortcomings of outcome-based budgeting, this approach is beneficial in tandem with the line-item approach (Brimley et al. 2020).

Regardless of the specific budgetary methodology, the budget officer and staff should identify and record actual revenue by category from the previous 2 years as a historical perspective to estimate revenue for an upcoming fiscal year. The budget official estimates revenues, including unencumbered carryover fund balances from the previous year, and checks percentage changes (Wood et al., 2019).

After logging the previous revenue for 2 years, the budget official estimates the upcoming fiscal year's revenue based on assumptions and historical trends. An assumption describes any precondition that the budget officer considers when developing the budget and should be absolute before budgeting, especially for state basic aid, federal funding, and student enrollment (Wood et al., 2019). For instance, when unrestricted grants-in-aid (i.e., state basic aid) historically increased 3 percent each of the last 3 years, then the assumption is the annual percentage change will be 3 percent to estimate future dollars. Table 5.4 illustrates a general fund document for estimating budget revenue.

The practice of envisioning seeks to maintain, improve, or diminish the current school operation for deliberation on new initiatives (Wood et al., 2019). Depending on the chosen budgetary method, envisioning may proceed with differing actions to allocate dollars:

- Incremental line-item budgeting envisions program modifications through minor budgetary changes.

**Table 5.4.   General Fund Document for Estimating Revenue**

| General Fund | Actual Previous 2 Years | Actual Previous Year | Percentage Change | Funding Estimate | Notes |
|---|---|---|---|---|---|
| Unencumbered Cash Balance (Unrestricted Revenue) | | | | | |
| Unencumbered Cash Balance (Restricted Revenue) | | | | | |
| **Local Sources** | | | | | |
| Property Tax | | | | | |
| Local Sales Tax | | | | | |
| Local Income Tax | | | | | |
| Supplementary Tax | | | | | |
| Nontax Revenue—Tuition | | | | | |
| Nontax Revenue—User Fees | | | | | |
| Other: | | | | | |
| **State Sources** | | | | | |
| Unrestricted Grants-in-Aid | | | | | |
| Restricted Grants-in-Aid | | | | | |
| Other: | | | | | |
| **Federal Sources** | | | | | |
| Title I | | | | | |
| Title II | | | | | |
| Title III | | | | | |
| Title IV | | | | | |
| Title V | | | | | |
| Title VI | | | | | |
| Title VII | | | | | |
| IDEA Part B | | | | | |
| School Meal Programs | | | | | |
| Career and Technical Education | | | | | |
| School-based Medicare | | | | | |
| Other: | | | | | |

- Zero-based budgeting foresees program changes through evaluation of each expenditure with zero dollars to start the process.
- Site-based budgeting visualizes program decisions at the site level.
- Performance-based budgeting solely imagines future monetary allotments via program performance.

Regardless of how the school district staff members assess programs, the underlying point remains that programs cost money; therefore, identifying program needs and expenditures for an annual budget is essential to translate action into fiscal terms. When program maintenance is the administrative goal, the district then should contemplate prior years' data trends as the baseline and utilize an incremental line-item budgeting approach.

When district management covets spending decisions at the lowest school level, site-based budgeting then should result to envision expenses. When district officials desire school improvement based on performance indicators, decision makers should employ performance-based budgeting. When district officials aspire to examine each operational aspect or a specific program from the bottom, a zero-based budgeting process then would be best (Brimley et al., 2020). In reality, a district may choose a blend of these processes to envision future expenses.

To estimate total expenditures for an annual budget, the incremental line-item method, as explained earlier, is the most popular and easiest to explain. Estimating general fund expenditures creates the best upcoming budget year approximations and projects major categories as follows:

- employee salaries, wages, and benefits;
- number of necessary employment positions;
- movement of each staff member on the applicable salary schedule;
- maintenance and daily operational costs;
- quantities and costs of supplies, equipment, and services (i.e., professional development, security, contract, and information technology); and
- student enrollment.

Salaries and benefits shape the largest expenditures for the district, which typically accounts for 70 to 80 percent of the budget. The budget officer should examine past salary and benefit costs to uncover trends. To project these costs for an annual budget, the payroll or human resources department should list current employees with salary estimates. Salary schedules and collective bargaining agreements, when mandated, assign the pay rates for the upcoming year.

Salaries and benefits correlate with projected student enrollment. When the district's student population significantly increases or decreases, projections become even more pronounced on the envisioned budget, especially salary and benefit expenses. An expanding student population burdens past budgets and may necessitate additional staff members.

To the contrary, when student enrollment declines, the district may need to reduce the staff, although often difficult with applied collective bargaining agreements. When student membership remains constant for a number of years, the student enrollment projection has less effect on the budget than in past years, with a rapidly rising or dwindling student population.

By example, when salaries increase by 3 percent in each of the past 3 years due to the changing salary schedule with no significant changes in the collective bargaining agreement, then a safe assumption is the district salary expense will once again increase by 3 percent, when the number of employees remain constant.

To estimate employee benefit costs for an annual budget, the budget officer must review the personnel policies adopted by the governing board and collective bargaining agreements, when mandated. To predict health care benefit costs, school officials should review current policies and programs and apply projected rates to the probable composition of next year's workforce. If health care benefits increased by 10 percent in each of the past 3 years, a safe assumption is the benefit will increase another 10 percent for the upcoming fiscal year.

To approximate retirement benefit expenses, school officials should employ projected rates for employer contributions to the state retirement system. To project workers' compensation expenditures, school officials should review current policies and past yearly expense histories. To anticipate the employer's share for Social Security benefits, school officials should apply the appropriate rate to the anticipated salary outlay for the next year (Office of the New York State Comptroller, 2019).

Other district expenses, such as purchased services, utilities (e.g., natural gas, electricity, and fuel), materials and supplies, capital outlay, and maintenance supply budget data. Table 5.5 shows a document to perform an estimated general fund incremental line-item budget by expenditure object.

Reliable revenue and expenditure forecasts are essential starting points for developing a balanced budget. All states require districts to balance budgets and forbid deficit spending. When expenditure estimates exceed revenue projections, the budget officer or school officials must adjust budgetary lines by increasing revenue or reducing expenditures. Because state and federal legislators set state and federal revenues respectively, local school

**Table 5.5. General Fund Document for Estimating Expenditures by Object**

| Object | Actual Previous 2 Years | Actual Previous Year | Percentage Change | Budget Based on Change Percentage | Assumptions and Notes |
|---|---|---|---|---|---|
| Salaries | | | | | |
| Employee Benefits | | | | | |
| Professional Services | | | | | |
| Purchased Services | | | | | |
| Student Transportation | | | | | |
| Supplies | | | | | |
| Capital Outlay | | | | | |
| Other | | | | | |

officials have little input to generate additional funding from these sources. However, to boost local monies, districts in 33 states may seek voter approval to increase local taxes above statutory limits as explained in chapter 2 (Ballotpedia, 2019b).

Maintaining a positive cash balance with reserves in unrestricted general fund accounts hedges against future unexpected expenses. In determining the proper reserve level, a district should analyze the risks facing the district and establish reserve levels commensurate with those risks (Wood et al., 2019).

Reducing budget expenditures, most often, remains easier than increasing revenue. Balancing the budget through expenditure reductions often create cause-and-effect circumstances. Personnel reductions are never easy, and many districts and school boards cut administrative and auxiliary staff before instructional staff. In times of severe budget shortfalls, however, teacher reduction is unavoidable (Odden & Picus, 2020).

After achieving a balanced budget, the budget still needs final approval. The final budget approval process differs across states, but the result is a legally adopted budget (see appendix-exhibit 1). In states with fiscally dependent school districts, the parent government must authorize the budget.

For independent school districts, each state specifies distinctive procedures for official budget summary notification, waiting period, public hearing, formal adoption of the tentative/proposed budget (see appendix-exhibit 2), and certification prior to final approval by the governing board at a regular board meeting. This process intends to guard against secrecy and impropriety (Wood et al., 2019). For a general calendar of budget activity, see table 5.3.

## APPROPRIATIONS

The adopted operating budget serves as a guide for expenditure allocations; however, the appropriation specifies the actual dollars appropriated in each account line. To develop the appropriation, decision makers must further detail spending in specific accounts, showing the appropriated line-item monies along with encumbered, expended, and unencumbered balances (Office of New York State Comptroller, 2019).

The previously mentioned standardized state codes pinpoint the detailed line-item appropriations. School districts may not incur expenditures unless the district appropriates dollars for that particular purpose. States and school districts across the country have various requirements for developing, approving, and filing appropriations in accord with specific buildings, subject areas, and job assignments (Odden & Picus, 2020).

Regardless of the method to allocate appropriation line-item amounts, the governing board must pass a resolution to approve the appropriation before the start of the fiscal year. A school board in Ohio must pass a temporary appropriation resolution by July 1 to meet the ordinary expenses of the district, until approving the permanent annual appropriation resolution. Ohio school boards, by state law, must adopt a permanent appropriation resolution before January 1. Appropriation modifications to the initial appropriation occur frequently throughout the fiscal year and oblige school board approval (Ohio Department of Education, 2018).

Upon appropriation approval, the superintendent, program supervisors, principals, and department heads monitor their supervised accounts. Transfers or modifications within the general fund appropriation lines are often necessary during the fiscal year for unexpected expenses. The superintendent, CFO/treasurer, program supervisor, or principal may initiate line-item transfer requests. The governing board must approve each transfer.

Because general fund monies are unrestricted, governing boards may authorize transfers of these fund dollars to restricted governmental funds (e.g., special revenue, debt service, and capital project). Governing boards, however, may not sanction restricted fund transfers into the general fund (Ohio Department of Education, 2018).

Before concluding the fiscal year, each line-item appropriation must balance, meaning that each line must have a zero or positive balance described as "being in the black" instead of a negative balance referred to as "being in the red." To finalize the appropriation, the CFO/treasurer presents the school board with the final appropriation that reflects all modifications to balance each line. Unencumbered monies in appropriated lines lapse at the conclusion of the fiscal year, although reserves may carry over to the next fiscal year.

## AUDITS

To protect a district from mismanagement, theft, unlawful transactions, and misuse, the school's accounting department must establish and maintain financial means (i.e., internal control) as well as evaluate and report fiscal practices. Internal control safeguards assets and verifies accuracy and reliability of accounting data through policies and procedures (Schandi & Foster, 2019). For example, a specific administrator should be accountable for each district account, expense, and revenue, so the information remains traceable.

For additional internal control, a sole individual should not possess complete authority over each transaction phase; thus, the person who prepares the purchase order should not also process the payment. In this manner, one employee checks the workflow of another employee (Schandi & Foster, 2019). For instance, at least two employees (e.g., superintendent and CFO/treasurer) should approve purchase orders before being processed.

Every school district should periodically audit accounts. The audit, an independent appraisal of district accounting, financial, and operational systems, investigates the record of accounts under the authority of the CFO/treasurer. This inspection verifies financial data and validates the lawful collection and utilization of funds in accordance with statutes and regulations.

Internal, state, and external audits are common types. District personnel who possess technical qualifications may conduct internal audits to assess the efficiency, appropriateness, and legality of a district's financial and accounting procedures.

To protect governmental financial interests, audits, conducted by state auditors, evaluate state and federal regulation compliance on selected accounts. Auditors assess all documentation related to state aid for general and categorical funding. With federal funds, the auditors assess program assurances, allowable activities, and expenditure reports. The nature and extent of these audits vary considerably by state. However, federal regulations mandate an annual audit for school districts that receive $750,000 or more in federal awards during a fiscal year (Office of Budget and Management, 2019).

Certified public accountants typically conduct end-of-the-year external audits to confirm cash balances, examine revenues and expenditures, verify physical inventories, validate fixed assets, review vendor obligations, inspect loan agreements, and substantiate district compliance in accord with the *Generally Accepted Accounting Principles*. To accomplish an external audit, the accountant examines board meeting minutes, receipt and expense verifications, ledger and payroll books of entry, inventories, insurance policies, trusts, and student activities (Brimley et al., 2020).

State and external audits must comply with Governmental Accounting Standards Board regulations. Allison (2015) reported the following financial statements that described a district's current and long-term financial status:

- A Statement of Net Position (see appendix-exhibit 8) depicts all the district's longstanding governmental and business activities by assets, liabilities, and total net financial position.
- A Statement of Activities (see appendix-exhibit 9) summarizes the current year's government and business revenues and expenses. This document simplifies financial data for a cost analysis of governmental and business (i.e., food service) activities.
- A Balance Sheet (see appendix-exhibit 10) illustrates a district's current financial data by fund.

- A Statement of Revenues, Expenditures, and Changes (see appendix-exhibit 4) focuses on immediate revenues and expenditures.

An external or state audit, without issues, yields an unqualified opinion because audit findings were not detected. On the other hand, when problems occur, the audit yields a qualified opinion with an audit finding, which is an auditor's conclusion of fact issued as a noncompliance citation, finding for adjustment, or finding for recovery (Ohio Auditor Office, 2018).

A noncompliance citation notes that the audit revealed a significant breach of a legal financial or contractual provision. A finding for adjustment compels the district to make an operational change. A finding for recovery means the audit unveiled a financial violation, and the violator must pay restitution (Wood et al., 2019).

For example, the Independent School District No. 273 in Minnesota violated state law, according to an audit. As a finding for adjustment, the audit obligated the district to pay vendors within 35 days after receipt of the goods or services (see appendix-exhibit 11). Boards of education review audit reports and must show receipt of an audit in board minutes.

Surety bonds, another vehicle to protect school funds, ensure the board of education that individuals involved in school business transactions fulfilled their duties within the law and guard the district against employee fraud or theft. When a financial loss occurs as a result of a fraudulent act on the part of a bonded employee, the bonding agency reimburses the district for the loss and pursues action against the individual to recover the money (Brimley et al., 2020).

## SUMMARY

Fund accounting, financial forecasting, budgeting, appropriating, and auditing describe district accounting services. By fund accounting, district staff members manage, record, and report revenue along with expenditures by assigned government accounts with standardized state account codes. School administrators should be able to read and interpret their state's account code string.

Forecasting, a vital accounting function, is not as precise as the annual budget; however, this long-range planning tool remains essential for future operations. Although Ohio is the only state that mandates financial forecasting, all states direct districts to create an annual budget.

Districts across the country differ regarding budget development approaches; however, research revealed four general methods: incremental line-item, zero-based, site-based, and performance-based. Many school districts employ variations of these strategies in common practice. Five interrelated activities (e.g., budget initialization, revenue estimation, educational program foresight, expenditure estimates, and budget balancing) are steps that school budget officers employ to create the typical budget.

Regardless of the methodology to develop the budget, the governing board must pass a resolution to approve an appropriation before the start of the fiscal year, with the purpose of authorizing expenditures. Auditing, the practice of maintaining financial controls, protects the district from mismanagement, theft, unlawful conversion, and misuse; verifies financial data; and certifies lawful revenue and expenditures.

## PROJECTS

1. Interview a CFO/treasurer or business administrator about the district accounting department and roles in the school operation. Report the findings.
2. Obtain a copy of your district's budget/appropriation and identify the fund structure for revenues and expenditures. Examine and describe each distinct fund that the district maintains.
3. Study a district's general fund accounts and identify the expenditures from each account.
4. Obtain a copy of your district/building monthly revenue and expenditure report, identify account codes, and explain a specific line.
5. Obtain a copy of your district's annual audit and report the findings.

# Appendix

**2018-2019 Final General Fund Budget**
**LEA : 122097502    Neshaminy SD**
Printed 7/2/2018 1:44:35 PM

<u>Amount</u>

**REVENUE FROM LOCAL SOURCES**

| | | |
|---|---|---|
| 6111 | Current Real Estate Taxes | 120,414,804 |
| 6112 | Interim Real Estate Taxes | 616,246 |
| 6113 | Public Utility Realty Taxes | 145,000 |
| 6114 | Payments in Lieu of Current Taxes - State / Local | 400,000 |
| 6120 | Current Per Capita Taxes, Section 679 | 197,661 |
| 6140 | Current Act 511 Taxes - Flat Rate Assessments | 378,241 |
| 6150 | Current Act 511 Taxes - Proportional Assessments | 5,589,908 |
| 6400 | Delinquencies on Taxes Levied / Assessed by the LEA | 2,904,000 |
| 6500 | Earnings on Investments | 1,046,014 |
| 6700 | Revenues from LEA Activities | 73,000 |
| 6800 | Revenues from Intermediary Sources / Pass-Through Funds | 1,553,882 |
| 6910 | Rentals | 712,272 |
| 6940 | Tuition from Patrons | 559,393 |
| 6990 | Refunds and Other Miscellaneous Revenue | 112,000 |

**REVENUE FROM LOCAL SOURCES**  **$134,702,421**

**REVENUE FROM STATE SOURCES**

| | | |
|---|---|---|
| 7110 | Basic Education Funding | 13,522,236 |
| 7160 | Tuition for Orphans Subsidy | 40,000 |
| 7271 | Special Education funds for School-Aged Pupils | 6,413,936 |
| 7292 | Pre-K Counts | 245,650 |
| 7311 | Pupil Transportation Subsidy | 1,261,640 |
| 7320 | Rental and Sinking Fund Payments / Building Reimbursement Subsidy | 611,560 |
| 7330 | Health Services (Medical, Dental, Nurse, Act 25) | 180,000 |
| 7340 | State Property Tax Reduction Allocation | 3,591,251 |
| 7505 | Ready to Learn Block Grant | 564,188 |
| 7810 | State Share of Social Security and Medicare Taxes | 3,005,219 |
| 7820 | State Share of Retirement Contributions | 13,182,206 |

**REVENUE FROM STATE SOURCES**  **$42,617,886**

**REVENUE FROM FEDERAL SOURCES**

| | | |
|---|---|---|
| 8514 | NCLB, Title I - Improving the Academic Achievement of the Disadvantaged | 655,548 |
| 8515 | NCLB, Title II - Preparing, Training and Recruiting High Quality Teachers and Principals | 190,772 |
| 8516 | NCLB, Title III - Language Instruction for Limited English Proficient and Immigrant Students | 18,436 |
| 8517 | NCLB, Title IV - 21St Century Schools | 17,908 |
| 8690 | Other Restricted Federal Grants-in-Aid Through the Commonwealth of PA | 260,950 |

Page

**Exhibit 1.   Neshaminy School District, Pennsylvania: FY 2019 General Fund Budget**
*Source:* Neshaminy School District. (2018). *Final budget.* Langhorne, PA: Author.

**BUDGET OVERVIEW**
**REVENUE & OTHER SOURCES OF FUNDING BUDGET**
**2019-20 Proposed Budget**

| | Actual 2015-16 | Actual 2016-17 | Actual 2017-18 | Projected Actual 2018-19 | Proposed Budget 2019-20 |
|---|---|---|---|---|---|
| **REVENUE** | | | | | |
| **State Aid** | | | | | |
| Foundation Aid | 4,117,901 | 4,327,622 | 4,542,330 | 4,738,583 | 4,796,321 |
| BOCES Aid | 791,920 | 925,640 | 914,748 | 975,599 | 966,269 |
| High Cost Excess Cost | 32,818 | 120,648 | 37,561 | 180,040 | 137,491 |
| Private Excess Cost | 88,959 | 87,699 | 63,635 | 51,662 | 65,232 |
| Local Share of Educ Costs | | | | | |
| Software, Library & Textbook | 397,932 | 377,126 | 390,395 | 374,536 | 368,664 |
| Transportation | | 504,971 | 526,644 | 561,801 | 582,583 |
| GAP elimination (reduction in aid) | | | | | |
| Building Aid | 509,796 | 535,369 | 525,117 | 525,044 | 873,359 |
| Other State Aid: | | | | | |
| NYS EFC Waste Water Treatment Reimb. | 158,307 | 155,037 | 73,858 | 210,000 | 210,000 |
| Summer School Aid | | | | | |
| Special Legislative Grant | 45,822 | 88,174 | 86,826 | 90,000 | - |
| Prior Year Aid Adjustments | | | | | |
| **Total State Aid** | 6,143,455 | 7,122,286 | 7,161,114 | 7,707,265 | 7,998,919 |

**REVENUE, Continued**

| | Actual 2015-16 | Actual 2016-17 | Actual 2017-18 | Projected Actual 2018-19 | Proposed Budget 2019-20 |
|---|---|---|---|---|---|
| **Miscellaneous Receipts** | | | | | |
| Day School Tuition-Non Residents | 66,220 | 20,340 | 19,800 | - | - |
| Day School Tuition-Other Districts | 1,714,052 | 1,394,424 | 1,316,811 | 1,000,000 | 1,389,000 |
| Health Services-Other Districts | 157,408 | 189,139 | 236,992 | 98,904 | 160,000 |
| Westchester County Sales Tax | 1,506,300 | 1,527,114 | 1,631,499 | 1,600,000 | 1,550,000 |
| Medicare Part D Reimbursement | 400,148 | 654,996 | 732,399 | 379,119 | 486,737 |
| Rental of Property | 579,376 | 586,021 | 529,471 | 633,072 | 520,000 |
| Insurance Recoveries | 38,408 | | 33,343 | 95,354 | |
| Interest on Cash Deposits | 15,185 | 21,146 | 32,814 | 127,440 | 130,000 |
| Refund-Prior Year Expenses including BOCES | 303,944 | 329,301 | 422,511 | 313,152 | 216,000 |
| Inter Transfer to Debt | 100,000 | | | | |
| Other Miscellaneous Receipts | 357,994 | 255,986 | 302,864 | 198,946 | 35,000 |
| **Total Miscellaneous Receipts** | 5,239,035 | 4,978,467 | 5,258,504 | 4,445,987 | 4,486,737 |

**Exhibit 2. Bedford Central School District, New York: Proposed FY 2020 Budget Document**
*Source:* Bedford Central School District. (2019). *Proposed FY 2020 budget.* Kisco, NY: Author.

**GENERAL FUND - REVENUES**

|         |                                          | 2017-18<br>FINAL<br>BUDGET | 2018-19<br>PROPOSED<br>BUDGET |
|---------|------------------------------------------|---------------------------:|------------------------------:|
|         | **Real Property Tax Items**              |                            |                               |
| A1081   | Other Payments in Lieu of Taxes          | 182,000                    | **186,000**                   |
| A1090   | Interest Penalties - Real Property Tax   | 31,000                     | **33,000**                    |
|         |                                          | 213,000                    | 219,000                       |
|         | **Total Real Property Tax Items**        | 213,000                    | **219,000**                   |
|         | **Non Property Tax Items**               |                            |                               |
| A1111   | Tax on Consumers Utility Bills           | 325,000                    | **325,000**                   |
|         | **Total - Non Property Tax Items**       | 325,000                    | **325,000**                   |
|         | **Charges for Services**                 |                            |                               |
| A1410   | Admissions                               | 15,000                     | **12,000**                    |
| A2230   | Day School Tuition-Other Districts        | 33,000                     | **37,000**                    |
|         |                                          | 48,000                     | 49,000                        |
|         | **Total - Charges for Services**         | 48,000                     | **49,000**                    |
|         | **Use of Money and Property**            |                            |                               |
| A2401   | Interest & Earnings - General Accounts    | -                          | -                             |
| A2410   | Use of Buildings                         | 33,000                     | **25,000**                    |
|         | **Total Use of Money & Property**        | 33,000                     | **25,000**                    |
|         | **Miscellaneous**                        |                            |                               |
| A2701   | Refund of Prior Years Expenses           | 180,000                    | **180,000**                   |
| A2770   | Other Unclassified                       | 30,000                     | **30,000**                    |
|         |                                          | 210,000                    | 210,000                       |
|         | **Total - Miscellaneous**                | 210,000                    | **210,000**                   |

Exhibit 3.   Watervliet City School District, New York: Estimated Utility Tax Revenue

*Source:* Watervliet City Schools. (2018). *General fund-revenues.* Watervliet, NY: Author.

**Bexley City School District**
STATEMENT OF REVENUES, EXPENDITURES AND CHANGES
IN FUND BALANCES
GOVERNMENTAL FUNDS
FOR THE FISCAL YEAR ENDED JUNE 30, 2018

| | GENERAL | BOND RETIREMENT FUND | OTHER GOVERNMENTAL FUNDS | TOTAL GOVERNMENTAL FUNDS |
|---|---|---|---|---|
| REVENUES: | | | | |
| Property taxes | $ 19,236,843 | 1,173,415 | 561,140 | 20,971,398 |
| Income tax | 6,290,383 | - | - | 6,290,383 |
| Intergovernmental: | | | | |
| Federal Restricted Grants-in-aid | - | - | 909,260 | 909,260 |
| State: | | | | |
| Unrestricted Grants-in-aid | 7,330,541 | 207,791 | - | 7,538,332 |
| Restricted Grants-in-aid | - | - | 667,166 | 667,166 |
| Investment income | 248,603 | - | 31,737 | 280,340 |
| Co-curricular activities | 65,448 | - | 256,064 | 321,512 |
| Charges for services | - | - | 600,699 | 600,699 |
| Tuition fees | 117,066 | - | - | 117,066 |
| Other | 131,186 | - | 418,751 | 549,937 |
| TOTAL REVENUES | 33,420,070 | 1,381,206 | 3,444,817 | 38,246,093 |
| EXPENDITURES: | | | | |
| Current: | | | | |
| Instructional services: | | | | |
| Regular | 17,370,354 | - | 177,850 | 17,548,204 |
| Special | 4,724,682 | - | 497,438 | 5,222,120 |
| Vocational | 451,633 | - | - | 451,633 |
| TOTAL INSTRUCTIONAL SERVICES | 22,546,669 | - | 675,288 | 23,221,957 |
| Support services: | | | | |
| Operation and maintenance of plant | 3,779,022 | - | - | 3,779,022 |
| School administration | 2,530,894 | - | 35,897 | 2,566,791 |
| Instructional staff | 1,815,319 | - | - | 1,815,319 |
| Pupils | 1,946,291 | - | 188,105 | 2,134,396 |
| Business operations | 1,380,572 | 21,808 | 10,192 | 1,412,572 |
| Student transportation | 668,643 | - | - | 668,643 |
| Food services | - | - | 857,484 | 857,484 |
| Central services | 431,092 | - | - | 431,092 |
| General administration | 108,348 | - | - | 108,348 |
| TOTAL SUPPORT SERVICES | 12,660,181 | 21,808 | 1,091,678 | 13,773,667 |
| Co-curricular student activities | 1,037,334 | - | 338,799 | 1,376,133 |
| Community services | - | - | 867,886 | 867,886 |
| Capital outlay | 685,685 | - | 411,151 | 1,096,836 |
| Debt service: | | | | |
| Principal retirement | - | 1,195,000 | - | 1,195,000 |
| Interest | - | 353,725 | - | 353,725 |
| TOTAL EXPENDITURES | 36,929,869 | 1,570,533 | 3,384,802 | 41,885,204 |
| Excess (deficiency) of revenues over expenditures | (3,509,799) | (189,327) | 60,015 | (3,639,111) |
| OTHER FINANCING SOURCES (USES): | | | | |
| Transfers in | - | - | 206,000 | 206,000 |
| Transfers out | (206,000) | - | - | (206,000) |
| TOTAL OTHER FINANCING SOURCES (USES) | (206,000) | - | 206,000 | - |
| Net Change in Fund Balances | (3,715,799) | (189,327) | 266,015 | (3,639,111) |
| FUND BALANCES AT BEGINNING OF YEAR | 33,165,749 | 2,322,599 | 2,377,984 | 37,866,332 |
| FUND BALANCE AT END OF YEAR | $ 29,449,950 | 2,133,272 | 2,643,999 | 34,227,221 |

The notes to the basic financial statements are an integral part of this statement.

**Exhibit 4.** Bexley City School District, Ohio: Statement of Revenue, Expenditures, and Changes

*Source:* Bexley City Schools. (2019). *Statement of revenue, expenditures, and changes.* Bexley, OH: Author.

AMENDED OFFICIAL CERTIFICATE OF ESTIMATED RESOURCES
(SCHOOL)
Rev. Code, Sec. 5705.36

Office of the Budget Commission, Montgomery County, Ohio,

To the Board of the      **Dayton City School District:**

The following is the amended official certificate of estimated resources for the fiscal year beginning July 1st,      as revised by the Budget Commission of Montgomery County, which shall govern the total of appropriations made at any time during such fiscal year:

| Fund Type/ Classification | Unencumbered Balance July 01, 20 | Property Taxes (*) | Other Sources | Total |
|---|---|---|---|---|
| General Fund | $ 3,819,447.34 | $ 63,057,052.00 | $ 133,952,948.00 | $ 200,829,447.34 |
| Special Revenue | $ 4,981,347.79 | $ 726,765.00 | $ 69,144,373.07 | $ 74,852,485.86 |
| Debt Service | $ 14,493,982.24 | $ 14,405,094.00 | $ 1,408,516.06 | $ 30,307,592.30 |
| Capital Projects | $ 105,278,554.70 | $ 726,765.00 | $ 192,404,748.41 | $ 298,410,068.11 |
| Enterprise | $ (609,337.40) | $ - | $ 11,933,510.00 | $ 11,324,172.60 |
| Internal Service | $ 609,753.36 | $ - | $ 2,404,500.00 | $ 3,014,253.36 |
| Trust and Agency | $ 7,589,718.31 | $ - | $ 6,801,000.00 | $ 14,390,718.31 |
| Totals | $ 136,163,466.34 | $ 78,915,676.00 | $ 418,049,595.54 | $ 633,128,737.88 |

* Includes rollback & homestead

Signed _____

**Exhibit 5.   Dayton City School District, Ohio: Amended Certificate of Estimated Resources**

*Source:* Dayton City Schools. (2018). Amended certificate of estimated resources. Retrieved from https://www.dps.k12.oh.us/documents/Board_Meetings/2008/Att%201_04%2001%202008%20Cert%20of%20Est%20Resources%20FY08R.pdf.

District Type: Local
IRN: 069682
County: Guernsey
Date Submitted: 10/30/2018 Date Processed: 10/30/2018

| Line | Actual | | | Forecasted | | | | |
|---|---|---|---|---|---|---|---|---|
| | 2016 | 2017 | 2018 | 2019 | 2020 | 2021 | 2022 | 2023 |
| 1.010 General Property | 3,575,050 | 5,058,985 | 4,536,352 | 5,121,248 | 5,306,074 | 5,453,680 | 5,541,494 | 5,614,528 |
| 1.035 Unrestricted Grants-in-Aid | 6,125,328 | 6,076,463 | 6,079,415 | 6,040,087 | 6,063,410 | 6,062,446 | 6,062,900 | 6,063,218 |
| 1.040 Restricted Grants-in-Aid | 105,295 | 167,820 | 179,385 | 224,815 | 212,537 | 214,340 | 213,491 | 222,897 |
| 1.050 Property Tax Allocation | 416,476 | 403,883 | 371,467 | 402,305 | 408,486 | 410,685 | 417,248 | 422,710 |
| 1.060 All Other Operating Revenue | 1,349,251 | 1,669,051 | 1,965,441 | 2,004,750 | 2,044,845 | 2,085,742 | 2,127,457 | 2,170,006 |
| 1.070 Total Revenue | 11,571,400 | 13,376,202 | 13,132,060 | 13,793,205 | 14,035,352 | 14,226,893 | 14,362,590 | 14,493,359 |
| 2.040 Operating Transfers-In | 530 | | | 1,000 | 1,000 | 1,000 | 1,000 | 1,000 |
| 2.050 Advances-In | 93,793 | 41,080 | 22,843 | 25,000 | 25,000 | 25,000 | 25,000 | 25,000 |
| 2.060 All Other Financial Sources | 33,484 | | | 5,000 | 5,000 | 5,000 | 5,000 | 5,000 |
| 2.070 Total Other Financing Sources | 127,807 | 41,080 | 22,843 | 31,000 | 31,000 | 31,000 | 31,000 | 31,000 |
| 2.080 Total Revenues and Other Financing Sources | 11,699,207 | 13,417,282 | 13,154,903 | 13,824,205 | 14,066,352 | 14,257,893 | 14,393,590 | 14,524,359 |
| 3.010 Personnel Services | 4,978,415 | 5,367,553 | 6,000,144 | 6,199,324 | 6,367,468 | 6,540,173 | 6,717,562 | 6,899,762 |
| 3.020 Employees' Retirement/Insurance Benefits | 2,777,126 | 3,103,052 | 3,233,433 | 3,511,724 | 3,680,119 | 3,856,305 | 4,337,625 | 4,904,868 |
| 3.030 Purchased Services | 2,007,875 | 2,157,968 | 2,456,459 | 2,485,788 | 2,535,504 | 2,586,214 | 2,637,938 | 2,690,697 |
| 3.040 Supplies and Materials | 521,176 | 551,761 | 1,101,821 | 687,876 | 708,512 | 729,767 | 751,660 | 774,210 |
| 3.050 Capital Outlay | 16,660 | 27,923 | 26,818 | 27,354 | 27,901 | 28,459 | 29,028 | 29,609 |
| 4.010 Debt Service: All Principal (Historical) | 28,800 | 28,800 | 102,258 | | | | | |
| 4.050 Debt Service: Principal - HB 264 Loans | | | | 28,800 | 28,800 | 28,800 | 28,800 | 28,800 |
| 4.055 Debt Service: Principal - Other | | | | 74,240 | 74,240 | 74,240 | | |
| 4.060 Debt Service: Interest and Fiscal Charges | 11,589 | 10,567 | 10,330 | 8,568 | 7,560 | 6,552 | 5,544 | 5,544 |
| 4.300 Other Objects | 609,938 | 609,799 | 583,200 | 589,032 | 594,922 | 600,871 | 606,880 | 612,949 |
| 4.500 Total Expenditures | 10,951,579 | 11,857,423 | 13,514,463 | 13,612,706 | 14,025,026 | 14,451,381 | 15,115,037 | 15,946,439 |
| 5.010 Operational Transfers - Out | 63,007 | 53,117 | 222,025 | 75,000 | 75,000 | 75,000 | 75,000 | 75,000 |
| 5.020 Advances - Out | 41,080 | 21,043 | 14,185 | 25,000 | 25,000 | 25,000 | 25,000 | 25,000 |
| 5.040 Total Other Financing | 104,087 | 74,160 | 236,210 | 100,000 | 100,000 | 100,000 | 100,000 | 100,000 |
| 5.050 Total Expenditure and Other Financing Uses | 11,055,666 | 11,931,583 | 13,750,673 | 13,712,706 | 14,125,026 | 14,551,381 | 15,215,037 | 16,046,439 |
| 6.010 Excess Rev & Oth Financing Sources over(under) Exp & Oth Financing | 643,541 | 1,485,699 | (595,770) | 111,499 | (58,674) | (293,488) | (821,447) | (1,522,080) |
| 7.010 Beginning Cash Balance | 4,232,829 | 4,876,370 | 6,362,069 | 5,766,299 | 5,877,798 | 5,819,124 | 5,525,636 | 4,704,189 |
| 7.020 Ending Cash Balance | 4,876,370 | 6,362,069 | 5,766,299 | 5,877,798 | 5,819,124 | 5,525,636 | 4,704,189 | 3,182,109 |
| 8.010 Outstanding Encumbrances | 648,405 | 475,149 | 126,266 | 250,000 | 250,000 | 250,000 | 250,000 | 250,000 |
| 10.010 Fund Balance June 30 for Certification of Appropriations | 4,227,965 | 5,886,920 | 5,640,033 | 5,627,798 | 5,569,124 | 5,275,636 | 4,454,189 | 2,932,109 |
| 12.010 Fund Bal June 30 for Cert of Contracts,Salary Sched,Oth Obligations | 4,227,965 | 5,886,920 | 5,640,033 | 5,627,798 | 5,569,124 | 5,275,636 | 4,454,189 | 2,932,109 |
| 15.010 Unreserved Fund Balance June 30 | 4,227,965 | 5,886,920 | 5,640,033 | 5,627,798 | 5,569,124 | 5,275,636 | 4,454,189 | 2,932,109 |

**Exhibit 6.   East Guernsey Local School District, Ohio: Five-Year Forecast**

*Source:* Ohio Department of Education. (2019a). Five-year forecast: Traditional districts. Retrieved from http://education.ohio.gov/Topics/Finance-and-Funding/Five-Year-Forecasts/Five-Year-Forecast-Traditional-Districts.

| Account Code FUND-FUNC-OBJ-SCC-SUBJ-OU-IL-JOB | Description | FYTD Appropriated | Carry-over | FYTD Expendable | FYTD Actual Expenditures | Current Encumbrances | FYTD Unencumbered Balance | FYTD Percent Exp/Func |
|---|---|---|---|---|---|---|---|---|
| 001-1100-423-0000-000000-015-00-000 | Equipment Repair | $2,000 | 0 | $2,000 | 0 | 0 | $2,000 | 0 |
| 001-1100-447-0000-000000-015-00-000 | Internet | $6,0000 | 0 | $6,0000 | 0 | 0 | 0 | 0 |
| 001-1130-429-0000-000000-015-00-000 | Copier Lease | $15,000 | 0 | $15,000 | $16,488.10 | 0 | $1,488.10- | 109.92% |
| 001-1130-511-0000-000000-015-00-000 | Inst. Supplies | $20,000 | 0 | $20,000 | $6,128.20 | $591.55 | $13,280.25 | 33.60% |
| 001-1130-511-0000-000000-015-16-000 | Inst. Supplies | $8,500 | $125 | $8,625 | $352.42 | 0 | $8,272.58 | 4.47% |
| 001-1130-516-0000-000000-015-00-000 | Software | $6,000 | $200 | $6,200 | 0 | 0 | $6,200 | 0 |
| 001-1130-517-0000-120000-015-16-000 | Band Repair | $5,516.25 | 0 | $5,516.25 | $5,641.09 | $168 | $292.84- | 105.31% |
| 001-2223-849-0000-000000-015-00-000 | Audiovisual24 21 | $250 | 0 | $250 | 0 | 0 | $250 | 0 |
| 001-2421-443-0000-000000-015-00-000 | Postage | 0 | $865 | $865 | $1,511.67 | $61.20 | $707.87- | 182% |
| 001-2421-519-0000-000000-015-00-000 | Principal Supplies | 0 | $1,001 | $1,001 | $1,207.10 | $786.35 | $992.45- | 199% |
| 001-2700-453-0000-000000-015-00-000 | Propane | $40,000 | $3,000 | $40,000 | $35,071.21 | 0 | $7,928.79 | 81.56% |
| 001-2790-441-0000-000000-015-00-000 | Telephone | $6,0000 | $594 | $6,594 | $6,348.95 | $5,200 | $4,951.95- | 175.12% |
| 003-1100-640-0000-000000-000-00-000 | Instruction Equipment | $22,595.00 | 0 | $22,595.00 | $24,545.00 | 0 | $1,950.00- | 108.63% |
| 007-1990-881-9006-000000-000-00-000 | Scholarship | $5,000 | 0 | $5,000 | $2,500 | 0 | $2,500 | 50% |
| 018-2421-882-9015-000000-015-00-000 | Principal Fund (Awards) | $1,000 | 0 | $1,000 | 0 | 0 | $1,000 | 0 |
| 200-4610-510-9002-000000-015-00-000 | Honor Society | $1,725.00 | 0 | $1,725.00 | $1,736.97 | 0 | $11.97- | 100.69% |
| 200-4113-510-9140-000000-015-00-000 | Drama Club Supplies | $1,551.18 | 0 | $1,551.18 | $1,645.00 | 0 | $93.35- | 113.84% |
| 300-9100-000-0000-000000-000-00-000 | Athletic Fund | $118,365.00 | $2,935 | $121,300 | $93,078 | $5,836.97 | $16,385.03 | 87.5% |
| 466-3411-439-9014-000000-000-00-000 | Straight A Grant | $8,710.20 | 0 | $8,710.20 | 0 | 0 | $8,710.20 | 0 |
| 599-1100-500-9160-000000-000-00-000 | IDEA-Part B Supplies | $3,243.33 | 0 | $3,243.33 | 0 | 0 | $3,243.33 | 0 |

**Exhibit 7. Monthly Budget/Appropriation Account Summary**

*Source:* East Guernsey Local Schools. (2019). Monthly budget/appropriation account summary. Retrieved from http://eguernsey.k12.oh.us/.

| | Governmental Activities | Business-Type Activities | Total |
|---|---|---|---|
| **ASSETS** | | | |
| Cash and cash equivalents | $ 42,871,042 | $ 7,664,712 | $ 50,535,754 |
| Investments | 61,962,339 | 163,531 | 62,125,870 |
| Property taxes receivable (net) | 12,182,730 | — | 12,182,730 |
| Due from other governments | 19,968,336 | 2,002,921 | 21,971,257 |
| Other receivables | 3,688,518 | 4,081 | 3,692,599 |
| Internal balances | 615,597 | (615,597) | — |
| Inventories | 1,537,230 | 1,949,526 | 3,486,756 |
| Nondepreciated capital assets (Note 2) | 32,272,411 | — | 32,272,411 |
| Depreciated capital assets (Note 2) | 381,428,545 | 11,549,456 | 392,978,001 |
| Less: Accumulated depreciation | (98,176,725) | (9,016,026) | (107,192,751) |
| Total assets | 458,350,023 | 13,702,604 | 472,052,627 |
| **DEFERRED OUTFLOWS OF RESOURCES** | | | |
| Accumulated decrease in fair value of hedging derivatives | 1,754,896 | — | 1,754,896 |
| Total deferred outflows of resources | 1,754,896 | — | 1,754,896 |
| **LIABILITIES** | | | |
| Accounts payable and other current liabilities | 34,668,368 | 1,303,768 | 35,972,136 |
| Long-term obligations (Note 3) | | | |
| Due within one-year | | | |
| Bonds, capital leases, and contracts | 13,446,974 | — | 13,446,974 |
| Accrued interest | 759,880 | — | 759,880 |
| Other | 7,856,000 | — | 7,856,000 |
| Due beyond one-year | | | |
| Bonds, capital leases, and contracts | 70,958,588 | — | 70,958,588 |
| Accrued interest | 16,014,649 | — | 16,014,649 |
| Other | 23,082,406 | — | 23,082,406 |
| Total liabilities | 166,786,865 | 1,303,768 | 168,090,633 |
| **DEFERRED INFLOWS OF RESOURCES** | | | |
| Accumulated increase in fair value of hedging derivatives | 1,435,599 | — | 1,435,599 |
| Total deferred inflows of resources | 1,435,599 | — | 1,435,599 |
| **NET POSITION** | | | |
| Net investment in capital assets | 231,437,966 | 2,533,430 | 233,971,396 |
| Restricted for: | | | |
| Debt service | 4,133,180 | — | 4,133,180 |
| School-based activities | 1,396,569 | — | 1,396,569 |
| Unrestricted | 54,914,740 | 9,865,406 | 64,780,146 |
| Total net position | $ 291,882,455 | $ 12,398,836 | $ 304,281,291 |

**Exhibit 8.   Statement of Net Position**

*Source:* Allison, G. S. (2015). *Financial accounting for local and state school systems: 2014 edition* (NCES 2015-347). Washington, DC: U.S. Department of Education, National Center for Education Statistics.

| Functions/Programs | Expenses | Program Revenues | | | Net (Expense) Revenue and Changes in Net Position | | |
| | | Charges for Services | Operating Grants and Contributions | Capital Grants and Contributions | Primary Government | | |
| | | | | | Governmental Activities | Business-Type Activities | Total |
|---|---|---|---|---|---|---|---|
| Governmental activities: | | | | | | | |
| Instruction and instruction-related services | $ 238,876,955 | $ 5,509,719 | $ 27,631,301 | – | $ (205,735,935) | | $ (201,633,842) |
| Instructional and school leadership | 34,166,630 | – | 3,783,490 | – | (30,383,140) | | (29,796,417) |
| Support services—student-based | 37,963,791 | 2,986,172 | 4,203,974 | – | (30,773,645) | | (30,121,715) |
| Administrative support services | 9,528,781 | – | 1,055,183 | – | (8,473,598) | | (8,309,966) |
| Support services—nonstudent-based | 58,382,470 | – | 5,465,065 | – | (52,917,405) | | (51,914,837) |
| Community services | 2,801,454 | – | 131,297 | – | (2,670,157) | | (2,622,049) |
| Interest on long-term debt | 5,969,465 | – | – | – | (5,969,465) | | (5,969,465) |
| Total government activities | 387,689,545 | 8,495,891 | 42,270,310 | – | (336,923,344) | | (336,923,344) |
| Business-type activities: | | | | | | | |
| Food services | 20,596,032 | 4,750,350 | 15,849,235 | $ 750,000 | | $ 753,553 | 753,553 |
| Adult education | 1,837,753 | 936,150 | 1,102,491 | – | | 200,888 | 200,888 |
| Total business-type activities | 22,433,785 | 5,686,500 | 16,951,726 | 750,000 | | 954,441 | 954,441 |
| Total school district | $ 410,123,330 | $ 14,182,391 | $ 59,222,036 | $ 750,000 | (336,923,344) | 954,441 | (335,968,903) |
| General revenues: | | | | | | | |
| Taxes: | | | | | | | |
| Property taxes, levied for general purposes | | | | | 154,108,322 | – | 154,108,322 |
| Property taxes, levied for debt service | | | | | 16,860,557 | – | 16,860,557 |
| State aid—formula grants | | | | | 176,265,211 | – | 176,265,211 |
| Investment earnings | | | | | 7,397,103 | 312,271 | 7,709,374 |
| Special item—gain on sale of unimproved land | | | | | 1,367,341 | – | 1,367,341 |
| Total general revenues and special item | | | | | 355,998,534 | 312,271 | 356,310,805 |
| Change in net position | | | | | 19,075,190 | 1,266,712 | 20,341,902 |
| Net position—beginning | | | | | 272,487,968 | 11,132,124 | 283,620,092 |
| Net position—ending | | | | | $ 291,563,158 | $ 12,398,836 | $ 303,961,994 |

**Exhibit 9.  Statement of Activities**

*Source:* Allison, G. S. (2015). *Financial accounting for local and state school systems: 2014 edition* (NCES 2015-347). Washington, DC: U.S. Department of Education, National Center for Education Statistics.

| | General Fund | Debt Service Fund | Other Governmental Funds | Total |
|---|---|---|---|---|
| **ASSETS** | | | | |
| Cash and Cash Equivalents | $ 38,369,672 | $ 3,294,850 | $ 1,206,520 | $ 42,871,042 |
| Investments | 62,495,133 | — | 902,805 | 63,397,938 |
| Property taxes receivable, net | 10,341,512 | 1,841,218 | — | 12,182,730 |
| Due from other governments | 15,105,826 | — | 4,862,510 | 19,968,336 |
| Accrued interest | 504,757 | — | — | 504,757 |
| Due from other funds | 5,170,479 | 759,359 | 1,852,454 | 7,782,292 |
| Other receivables | 1,218,640 | 20,695 | 508,827 | 1,748,162 |
| Inventories—supplies and materials | 1,412,121 | — | — | 1,412,121 |
| Other current assets | 125,109 | — | — | 125,109 |
| Total assets | $ 134,743,249 | $ 5,916,122 | $ 9,333,116 | 149,992,487 |
| | | | | |
| **LIABILITIES AND FUND BALANCES** | | | | |
| Liabilities: | | | | |
| Accounts payable and accrued liabilities | $ 30,270,632 | $ 8,740 | $ 933,434 | $ 31,212,806 |
| Due to other funds | 20,845,752 | — | $ 5,503,492 | 26,349,244 |
| Due to other governments | 10,093 | — | — | 10,093 |
| Due to student groups | — | — | 256,183 | 256,183 |
| Deferred revenue | 12,283,000 | 1,774,202 | 1,243,438 | 15,300,640 |
| Amounts held for granting agencies | 233,035 | — | — | 233,035 |
| Total liabilities | 63,642,512 | 1,782,942 | 7,936,547 | 73,382,001 |
| Fund balances: | | | | |
| Nonspendable: Inventories | 1,412,121 | — | — | 1,412,121 |
| Restricted for: | | | | |
| Debt service | — | 4,133,180 | — | 4,133,180 |
| Early childhood programs | 3,161,173 | — | — | 3,161,173 |
| Committed to: | | | | |
| Classroom technology | | | 333,000 | 333,000 |
| Athletic facilities | | | 1,250,000 | 1,250,000 |
| Assigned to: | | | | |
| New middle school contruction | — | — | 21,347,665 | 21,347,665 |
| Extended day program | | | 1,396,569 | 1,396,569 |
| Unassigned | 43,596,778 | — | — | 43,596,778 |
| Total fund balances | 48,170,072 | 4,133,180 | 24,327,234 | 76,630,486 |
| Total liabilities and fund balances | $ 111,812,584 | $ 5,916,122 | $ 32,263,781 | |

**Exhibit 10. Governmental Funds Balance Sheet**

*Source:* Allison, G. S. (2015). *Financial accounting for local and state school systems: 2014 edition* (NCES 2015-347). Washington, DC: U.S. Department of Education, National Center for Education Statistics.

**CLAIMS AND DISBURSEMENTS**

**Criteria** – Minnesota Statute § 471.425, Subd. 2.

**Condition** – Minnesota Statutes require districts to pay each vendor obligation according to the terms of each contract or within 35 days after the receipt of the goods or services or the invoice for the goods or services. If such obligations are not paid within the appropriate time period, Independent School District No. 273, Edina, Minnesota (the District) must pay interest on the unpaid obligations at the rate of 1.5 percent per month or part of a month. For one disbursement tested, the District did not pay the obligation within the required time period, and did not pay interest on the unpaid obligation.

**Questioned Costs** – Not applicable.

**Context** – One of forty disbursements tested were not in compliance. This is a current year and prior year finding.

**Effect** – Certain payments made to vendors were not paid within the timeframe as required by state statute, and the vendors were not paid interest to which they were entitled.

**Cause** – All general disbursement invoices are paid through the district office. Invoices must be approved by the appropriate personnel at the school and/or department that received the goods or services prior to payment. On occasion, there is a timing delay in obtaining the necessary approval for payment and returning the invoice to the district office for payment.

**Recommendation** – We recommend that the District review claims and disbursement payment procedures in place to ensure future compliance with this statute.

**Corrective Action Plan**

**Actions Planned** – The District will review the payment procedures and will properly pay all invoices within the 35-day time limit.

**Official Responsible** – District Controller.

**Exhibit 11.   Independent School District No. 273, Minnesota: Audit Finding**

*Source:* Independent School District No. 273. (2016). Retrieved from http://perhamschools.org/wp-content/uploads/2018/06/2016.0549.01.Perham.FinStm.District.pdf.

# References

AASA, The School Superintendents Association. (2019a). Code of ethics. Retrieved from https://aasa.org/content.aspx?id=1390.

AASA, The School Superintendents Association. (2019b). *Structural inefficiencies in the school-based Medicaid program disadvantage small and rural districts and students*. Alexandria, VA: Author.

Afterschool Snack Program, 7 C.F.R. §226.17 (2010).

*Agostini v. Felton*, 521 U.S. 203 (1997).

Agriculture Adjustment Act, 7 U.S.C. 26 §§601 et seq. (1933).

*Aguilar v. Felton*, 473 U.S. 402 (1985).

Alexander, K., & Alexander, F. K. (2019). *American public school law* (9th ed.). St. Paul, MN: West Academic.

All Handicapped Children Act, 20 U.S.C. §1411 (1975).

Allison, G. S. (2015). *Financial accounting for local and state school systems: 2014 edition* (NCES 2015-347). Washington, DC: U.S. Department of Education, National Center for Education Statistics.

Appraisal Foundation. (2019). *Uniform standards of professional appraisal practice 2020–21* edition. Washington, DC: Author.

Art. of Conf. (1781).

Association for Career and Technical Education. (2018). *Legislative summary and analysis: Strengthening Career and Technical Education for the 21st Century Act (Perkins V)*. Alexandria, VA: Author.

Auditor of State. (2013). *Uniform school accounting system: User manual*. Columbus, OH: Author.

Ballotpedia. (2019a). Auditor. Retrieved from https://ballotpedia.org/Auditor.

Ballotpedia. (2019b). School bond and tax elections. Retrieved from https://ballotpedia.org/Voting_on_school_bond_and_tax_measures.

Bedford Central School District. (2019). *Proposed fy 2020 budget*. Kisco, NY: Author.

Bell, K. (2019, March 8). State taxes: Hawaii. Retrieved from https://www.bankrate.com/finance/taxes/state-taxes-hawaii.aspx.

Bexley City Schools. (2019). *Statement of revenue, expenditures, and changes*. Bexley, OH: Author.

Bivin, D., Osili, U., Pruitt, A., Bergdoll, J., Skidmore, T., Zarins, S., & Kou, X. (2018). *The philanthropy outlook 2018 and 2019*. Indianapolis: Indiana University Lilly Family School of Philanthropy.

*Board of Education v. Allen*, 392 U.S. 236 (1968).

Borders, M. A. (2018). The future of state Blaine amendments in light of Trinity Lutheran: Strengthening the nondiscrimination argument. *Notre Dame Law Review*, *93*(5), 2142–68.

Bowman, A. O., & Kearney, R. (2017). *State and local government*. Boston, MA: Cengage.

Brien, S. T. (2018). Strategic interaction among overlapping local jurisdictions. *The American Review of Public Administration*, *48*(6), 584–95.

Brimley, V., Verstegen, D. A., & Knoeppel, R. C. (2020). *Financing education in a climate of change* (13th ed.). Boston, MA: Pearson.

Cammanga, J. (2019). *State and local sales tax rates 2019* (No. 633). Washington, DC: Tax Foundation.

Carl D. Perkins Career and Technical Education Act, 20 U.S.C. §§2301 et seq. (2006).

Center on Budget and Policy Priorities. (2019a). *Policy basics: Introduction to the federal budget process*. Washington, DC: Author.

Center on Budget and Policy Priorities. (2019b). *Policy basics: Where do federal tax revenues come from?* Washington, DC: Author.

Center on Budget and Policy Priorities. (2019c, January 29). Policy basics: Where do federal tax revenues go? Retrieved from https://www.cbpp.org/research/federal-budget/policy-basics-where-do-our-federal-tax-dollars-go.

Center on Standards and Assessment Implementation. (2019, August 2). Consolidated state plans. Retrieved from https://www.csai-online.org/spotlight/consolidated-state-plans.

Child Nutrition Act, 7 U.S.C. §§1771-1985 (1966).

Civitas Institute. (2018). *North Carolina budget and tax highlights*. Raleigh, NC: Author.

Congressional Budget and Impoundment Control Act, 2 U.S.C. §§601-688 (1974).

Congressional Research Service. (2019a). *Child nutrition programs: Current issues* (CRS Report No. R45486). Washington, DC: Author.

Congressional Research Service. (2019b). *Federal grants to state and local governments: A historical perspective on contemporary issues* (CRS Report No. R40638). Washington, DC: Author.

Congressional Research Service. (2019c). *Social security primer* (CRS Report No. R42035). Washington, DC: Author.

Congressional Research Service. (2019d). *The Individuals with Disabilities Education Act (IDEA) funding: A primer* (CRS Report No. R44624). Washington, DC: Author Redacted.

Council for American Private Education. (2016). *Private schools and the Every Student Succeeds Act*. Germantown, MD: Author.

County Commissioners Association of Ohio. (2019). *2019–2020 legislative platform*. Columbus, OH: Author.

County Technical Assistance Service. (2019). *Local option sales tax*. Nashville: The University of Tennessee.

Daughtery, W., Hester, W. & Weatherill, K. (2016). *Tuition trends in independent day schools*. Nashville, TN: Peabody College of Vanderbilt University.

Dayton City Schools. (2018). Amended certificate of estimated resources. Retrieved from https://www.dps.k12.oh.us/documents/Board_Meetings/2008/Att%201_04 %2001%202008%20Cert%20of%20Est%20Resources%20FY08R.pdf.

Department of Legislative Services. (2018). *Overview of Maryland local governments: Finances and demographic information*. Annapolis, MD: Author.

Dunn, J. (2018). Narrow opening for school choice: But Blaine amendments stand, for now. *Education Next, 18*(1), 7.

East Guernsey Local School District.

EdChoice. (2019). *The ABC's of school choice: 2019 edition*. Indianapolis, IN: Author.

Education Commission of the States. (2018a, January). 50-state comparison-Charter schools: Does the state specify who must provide transportation to charter school students? Retrieved from http://ecs.force.com/mbdata/mbquestNB2C?rep=CS1707.

Education Commission of the States. (2018b, January). 50-state comparison-Charter schools: How is the funding for a charter school determined? Retrieved from http://ecs.force.com/mbdata/mbquestNB2C?rep=CS1716.

Education Commission of the States. (2018c, January). 50-state comparison-Charter schools: What organizations may authorize charter schools, and is there a statewide authorizing body? Retrieved from http://ecs.force.com/mbdata/mbquest NB2C?rep=CS1708.

Education Commission of the States. (2018d, January). 50-state comparison-Charter schools: What kind of facilities funding is available to charter schools? Retrieved from http://ecs.force.com/mbdata/mbquestNB2C?rep=CS1719.

Education Commission of the States. (2019, March). 50-state comparison-K–12 special education funding. Retrieved from https://www.ecs.org/50-state-comparison -k-12-special-education-funding/.

Education for All Handicapped Children Act, 20 U.S.C. §§1401 et seq. (1975).

Elementary and Secondary Education Act, 20 U.S.C. §§6301 et seq. (1965).

Erwin, B. (2019, April 18). *Interactive guide to school choice*. Retrieved from http://www.ncsl.org/research/education/interactive-guide-to-school-choice.aspx.

*Everson v. Board of Education*, 330 U.S. 1 (1947).

Every Student Succeeds Act, 20 U.S.C. §6301 (2015).

Food Research and Action Center. (2019). *Building strong school nutrition programs: A guide for charter schools*. Washington, DC: Author.

Forecast5 Analytics. (2019). Access your district's data story. Retrieved from https://www.forecast5analytics.com/5sight-story-offer.

Fruit and Vegetable Program, 7 C.F.R. §§211 & 235 (2010).

Geever, J. (2017). *Guide to proposal writing* [Audiobook]. New York: The Foundation Center.

Gillette, L., & Meyertholen, P. (n.d.). *The history and purpose of the migrant education program* [PowerPoint presentation]. Retrieved from https://results-assets

.s3.amazonaws.com/adm2019/2018%20NDO%20-%20The%20History%20and %20Purpose%20of%20the%20MEP%20508.pdf.

Grants.gov. (n.d.). How to apply for grants. Retrieved from https://www.grants.gov/ web/grants/applicants/apply-for-grants.html.

Hall, J. C., & Koumpias, A. M. (2016). *Growth and variability of school district income tax revenues: Is tax base diversification a good idea for school financing?* (Working Paper No. 15-14). Morgantown: West Virginia University College of Business and Economics.

Hawaii Department of Education. (2019a). *The budget: Fiscal year 2019–20*. Honolulu, HI: Author.

Hawaii Department of Education. (2019b). *Weighted student formula official enrollment allocation: Fiscal year 2019–20*. Honolulu, HI: Author.

Healthy, Hunger-Free Kids Act, 42 U.S.C. §1751 (2010).

Hinman, B. (2012). *The scoop on school and work in colonial America*. North Mankato, MN: Capstone Press.

Home School Legal Defense Association. (2019). *State laws concerning participation of homeschool students in public school activities*. Purcellville, VA: Author.

House Committee on Appropriations. (2019, April 29). Appropriations committee releases fiscal year 2020 Labor-HHS-Education Funding Bill. Retrieved from https:// appropriations.house.gov/news/press-releases/appropriations-committee-releases -fiscal-year-2020-labor-hhs-education-funding.

Illinois State Board of Education. (2019). *Overview of child nutrition programs*. Springfield, IL: Author.

Illinois Statewide School Management Alliance. (2018). *Programs for Illinois school districts*. Springfield, IL: Author.

Independent School District No. 273. (2016). Retrieved from http://perhamschools .org/wp-content/uploads/2018/06/2016.0549.01.Perham.FinStm.District.pdf.dayt.

Indian Education Formula Grants to Local Educational Agencies, 34 C.F.R. §§75, 77, 79, 81, 82, 84, 97, 98, & 99 (2017).

Individuals with Disabilities Education Act, 20 U.S.C. §§1400 et seq. (1990, 2004, 2015).

Iowa School Boards Association. (2018). *FY 2019 income surtax funding by school district*. Des Moines, IA: Association of School Boards Association.

Izard, R. (2019). *How federal programs support private k–12 students and teachers*. Denver, CO: Independence Institute.

Lapkoff & Gobalet Demographic Research, Inc. (2018). *Demographic analyses and enrollment forecasts: San Francisco Unified School District*. Saratoga, CA: Author.

Learning Landscape. (2016, June 21). Chapter 6: Philanthropy in k–12 education. Retrieved from https://thelearninglandscape.org/philanthropy-in-k-12-education/.

Legislative Analyst's Office. (2012). *Understanding California's property taxes*. Sacramento, CA: Author.

*Lemon v. Kurtzman*, 403 U.S. 602 (1971).

Lincoln Institute of Land Policy. (2018, October 4). Property tax in detail. Retrieved from https://www.lincolninst.edu/research-data/data-toolkits/significant-features -property-tax-state-state-property-tax-glance/property-tax-in-detail.

Local Government Commission. (2017). *Pennsylvania legislator's municipal desk-book* (5th ed.). Harrisburg, PA: Author.

Local Tax Enabling Act, 53 Pa. C. S. §§6901 et seq. (1965).

Locatelli, G., Mariani, G., Sainati, T., & Greco, M. (2017). Corruption in public projects and megaprojects: There is an elephant in the room! *International Journal of Project Management, 35*(3), 252–68.

Loughead, K., Walczak, J., & Bishop-Henchman, J. (2019). *Wisconsin tax options: A guide to fair, simple, pro-growth reform*. Washington, DC: Tax Foundation.

Loughead, K., & Wei, E. (2019). *State individual income tax rates and brackets for 2019*. Washington, DC: Tax Foundation.

Lueken, M. F., & Shuls, J. V. (2019). *The future of k–12 funding: How states can equalize and make k–12 funding more equitable*. Indianapolis, IN: EdChoice.

Maryland Association of Counties. (2019). *Budgets, tax rates, and selected statistics fiscal year 2019*. Annapolis, MD: Author.

Maurice, A., Russo, R., FitzSimmons, C., & Furtado, K. (2019). *Community eligibility: The key to hunger-free schools*. Washington, DC: Food Research and Action Center.

Maxwell, R. E., & Sweetland, S. R. (2013). *Ohio school finance: A practitioner's guide* (5th ed.). Cincinnati, OH: Anderson Publishing Company.

McFarland, J., Hussar, B., Zhang, J., Wang, X., Wang, K., Hein, S., . . . Barmer, A. (2019). *The condition of education 2019* (NCES 2019-144). Washington, DC: National Center for Education Statistics.

Medicaid and CHIP Payment and Access Commission. (2018). *Issue brief*. Washington, DC: Author.

Medicare Catastrophic Coverage Act, 42 U.S.C. §1396 (1988).

Meltzer, E. (January 26, 2018). The Douglas County voucher case is finally over. Retrieved from https://chalkbeat.org/posts/co/2018/01/26/the-douglas-county-voucher-case-is-finally-over.

Michigan School Business Officials. (2019). Dynamic budget projections (DBP). Retrieved from https://www.msbo.org/dynamic-budget-projections-dbp.

Mikesell, J. L., & Kioko, S. N. (2018, July). *The retail sales tax in a new economy*. Paper presented at the Municipal Finance Conference, Washington, DC.

*Mitchell v. Helms*, 530 U.S. 793 (2000).

Montana Office of Public Instruction. (2019). *Montana American Indian student achievement data report*. Helena, MT: Author.

National Association of Secondary School Administrators. (2019a). *Title II—Preparing, training, and recruiting high-quality teacher, principals, and other school leaders*. Reston, VA: Author.

National Association of Secondary School Administrators. (2019b). *Title III—Language Instruction for English learner and immigrant students*. Reston, VA: Author.

National Association of Secondary School Administrators. (2019c). *Title IV—21st Century Schools*. Reston, VA: Author.

National Association of State Budget Officers. (2015). *Budget processes in the states*. Washington, DC: Author.

National Association of State Budget Officers. (2019). *Fiscal survey of the states*. Washington, DC: Author.

National Council on Teacher Quality. (2019, January). Collective bargaining law. Retrieved from https://www.nctq.org/contract-database/collectiveBargaining#map-7.

National Defense Education Act, 20 U.S.C. §§401-602 (1958).

National Education Association. (2019a). *House appropriations committee, fy 2020.* Washington, DC: Author.

National Education Association. (2019b). *Rankings of the states 2018 and estimates of school statistics 2019.* Washington, DC: Author.

National Policy Board for Educational Administration. (2018). National educational leadership preparation (NELP) program standards–Building level. Retrieved from http://www.npbea.org.

Neshaminy School District. (2018). *Final budget.* Langhorne, PA: Author.

Nevada Const. art. X, § 5. (2013).

*New Mexico Association of Nonpublic Schools v. Moses*, 137 U.S. 2325 (2017).

New York State Department of Education. (2019). *State aid to schools: A primer.* Albany, NY: Author.

No Child Left Behind Act, 20 U.S.C. §6319 (2001).

Norcross, E., & Gonzalez, O. (2018). *Ranking the states by fiscal condition.* Arlington, VA: Mercatus Center.

North Carolina Department of Public Instruction. (2018). *2018–19 Allotment policy manual: State formulas.* Raleigh, NC: Author.

North Carolina Department of Public Instruction. (2019a). *Highlights of the North Carolina public school budget.* Raleigh, NC: Author.

North Carolina Department of Public Instruction. (2019b, September 9). State allotments. Retrieved from http://www.ncpublicschools.org/fbs/allotments/state/.

Odden, A., & Picus, L. (2020). *School finance: A policy perspective* (6th ed.). New York: McGraw-Hill.

Office of Budget and Management. (2019). *Compliance supplement.* Washington, DC: Author.

Office of Innovation and Improvement. (2019a). State regulations of private and home schools. Retrieved from https://innovation.ed.gov/resources/state-nonpublic -education-regulation-map.

Office of Innovation and Improvement. (2019b). Charter schools. Retrieved from https://innovation.ed.gov/what-we-do/charter-schools/.

Office of the Assessor. (2019). *2018 annual report.* Sacramento, CA: Author.

Office of the New York State Comptroller. (2019). *School district accounting and reporting manual.* Albany, NY: Author.

Office of the State Superintendent of Education. (2019). *Report on the uniform per student funding formula.* Washington, DC: Author.

Ohio Auditor Office. (2018). *Ohio compliance supplement.* Columbus, OH: Author.

Ohio Department of Education. (2018). *New chief fiscal officer/treasurers guide to managing grants.* Columbus, OH: Author.

Ohio Department of Education. (2019a). Five-year forecast: Traditional districts. Retrieved from http://education.ohio.gov/Topics/Finance-and-Funding/Five-Year -Forecasts/Five-Year-Forecast-Traditional-Districts.

Ohio Department of Education. (February, 2019b). Payment in lieu of transportation [Memorandum]. Columbus, OH: Author.

Ohio House Bill 920, 33 Ohio Rev. Code §319.301 (1976).

Ohio School Boards Association. (2018). *Understanding school levies.* Columbus, OH: Author.

Omnibus Amendment, 53 Pa. C. S. §1385 (1998).

O'Neal-McElrath, T., Kanter, L., & English, L. (2019). *Winning grants step by step: The complete workbook for planning, developing, and writing successful proposals* (5th ed.). Hoboken, NJ: John Wiley & Sons, Inc.

Public School Forum. (2019). *2018 North Carolina education primer.* Raleigh, NC: Author.

Ravich, D. (2019). *The great school wars: A history of the New York City public schools* (2nd ed.). [Electronic Book]. Baltimore, MD: Johns Hopkins University.

Ray, B. D. (2019, January 7). Research facts on homeschooling. Retrieved from https://www.nheri.org/research-facts-on-homeschooling.

Redmond, J. (2018, December 15). What does it mean to pay property tax in arrears? Retrieved from https://pocketsense.com/mean-pay-property-taxes-arrears-4749.html.

Richard B. Russell National School Lunch Act, 42 U.S.C. §§1751 et seq. (1946).

Rooney, P. (2018). *Memorandum to state Title I directors* [Memorandum]. Washington, DC: U.S. Department of Education.

Sales Tax Handbook. (2019). Retrieved from http://www.salestaxhandbook.com/.

*San Antonio Independent School District v. Rodriguez,* 411 U.S. 1 (1973).

Schandi, A., & Foster, P. L. (2019). *Internal control-integrated framework: An implementation guide for the healthcare provider industry.* New York: Committee of Sponsoring Organizations of Treadway Commission.

Schilling, C. A., & Tomal, D. R. (2019). *School finance and business management: Optimizing fiscal, facility and human resources* (2nd ed.). New York: Rowman & Littlefield.

School Breakfast Program, 7 C.F.R. §§220 & 245 (1966).

SchoolFunding.Info. (2019). Overview of litigation history. Retrieved from http://schoolfunding.info/litigation-map.

Schoolhouse Connection. (2019). *Q&A from our inboxes.* Washington, DC: Author.

School Milk Program, 7 C.F.R. §215 (1954).

*Serrano v. Priest,* 5 Cal. 3d 584 (Cal. 1971).

Sherman, S. (June 13, 2019). *Kentucky tax law update.* Paper presented at the annual Kentucky Bar Association convention, Louisville, Kentucky.

Sioux Falls School District. (2019). *FY 2020 proposed budget.* Sioux Falls, SD: Author.

Smith, A. (2017a). *The solution to trenchant inequity in Texas public education: A funding system that puts students first* (Policy Brief 140). Los Angeles, CA: Reason Foundation.

Smith, G. H. (2017b). *New methods for projecting enrollments within urban school districts.* Doctoral dissertation, University of Iowa, Iowa City.

Snyder, T. D., de Brey, C. & Dillow, S. A. (2019). *Digest of education statistics, 2017* (NCES 2018-070). Washington, DC: National Center for Education Statistics.

Social Security Amendments, 42 U.S.C. §1305 (1965).

Sparkman, W. E. (1994). The legal foundations of public school finance. *Boston College Law Review, 35*(3), 569–95.

State and Local Transferability Act, 20 U.S.C. §7305 (2015).

State of New Jersey Department of Education. (2019). Retrieved from https://www.nj.gov/cgi-bin/education/grants/gropps2.pl?string=recnum=01792&maxhits=1.

Strengthening Career and Technical Education for the 21st Century Act, 20 U.S.C. §§2399 et seq. (2018).

*Taxpayers for Public Education v. Douglas County School District*, 137 U.S. 232 (2017).

Telecommunications Act, 47 U.S.C. §§609 et seq. (1996).

Texas Education Agency. (2019a). *Financial accountability system resource guide.* Austin, TX: Author.

Texas Education Agency. (2019b). *2019-20 Summary of finances. Aransas Pass ISD.* Austin, TX: Author.

*Trinity Lutheran Church of Columbia, Inc. v. Comer*, 582 U.S. (2017).

Universal Service Administrative Company. (2019). *Schools and libraries (E-rate) program.* Washington, DC: Author.

U.S. Census Bureau. (2019a, May 2). Annual survey of state government finances tables, 2017. Retrieved from https://www.census.gov/programs-surveys/school-finances/newsroom/updates/fy-2017.html.

U.S. Census Bureau. (2019b). *Census of governments: Individual state descriptions 2017.* Washington, DC: Author.

U.S. Census Bureau. (2019c). *Form F-33: 2019 Census of governments survey of school system finance.* Washington, DC: Author.

U.S. Const. (1789).

U.S. Const. amend. X. (1791).

U.S. Department of Agriculture. (2019a, March 20). National school lunch program. Retrieved from https://www.fns.usda.gov/nslp/nslp-fact-sheet.

U.S. Department of Agriculture. (2019b, March 20). Special milk program. Retrieved from https://www.fns.usda.gov/smp/smp-fact-sheet.

U.S. Department of Agriculture. (2019c, March 31). The school breakfast program. Retrieved from https://www.fns.usda.gov/sbp/fact-sheet.

U.S. Department of Education. (2017, March 21). About impact aid. Retrieved from https://www2.ed.gov/about/offices/list/oese/impactaid/whatisia.html.

U.S. Department of Education. (2018a, October 24). Improving basic programs operated by local educational agencies (Title I, Part A). Retrieved from https://www2.ed.gov/programs/titleiparta/index.html.

U.S. Department of Education. (2018b, August 20). Education for homeless children and youths grants for state and local activities. Retrieved from https://www2.ed.gov/programs/homeless/legislation.html.

U.S. Department of Education. (2018c, March 20). Small, rural school achievement program. Retrieved from https://www2.ed.gov/programs/reapsrsa/index.html.

U.S. Department of Education. (2019a). *Fiscal year 2020 budget summary and background information*. Washington, DC: Author.

U.S. Department of Education. (2019b, June 18). Migrant education—Basic state formula grants. Retrieved from https://www2.ed.gov/programs/mep/index.html.

U.S. Department of Education. (2019c). *Supplement not supplant under Title I, Part A of the Elementary and Secondary Act of 1956 as amended by the Every Child Succeeds Act*. Washington, DC: Author.

U.S. 639 (2002).

Vermont Agency of Education. (2019). *2020 budget book*. Barre, VT: Author.

Verstegen, D. A. (2018). A quick glance at school finance: A 50-state survey of school finance policies. Retrieved from https://schoolfinancesdav.wordpress.com.

Virginia Department of Education. (2018). *Spending handbook for Title I, Part A; Title II, Part A; Title III, Part A; and Title IV, Part A*. Richmond, VA: Author.

Walczak, J. (2019). *Local income tax in 2019* (No. 667). Washington, DC: Tax Foundation.

Walczak, J., Kaeding, N. K., & Drenkard, S. (2018). *Pennsylvania: A 21st century tax code for the commonwealth*. Washington, DC: Tax Foundation.

Watervliet City Schools. (2018). *General fund-revenues*. Watervliet, NY: Author.

Weiner, K. G., & Green, P. C. (2018). *Private school vouchers: Legal challenges and civil rights protections* (Working Paper). Los Angeles, CA: UCLA Civil Rights Project.

West Virginia Department of Education. (2019a). *Executive summary of the public school support program*. East Charleston, WV: Author.

West Virginia Department of Education. (2019b). *Final computations: Public school support program for the 2018–19 year*. East Charleston, WV: Author.

Wisconsin Department of Public Instruction. (2019). *Certification of general aid: 2019–20 Marshall Public School District*. Madison, WI: Author.

Wood, R. C., Thompson, D. C., & Crampton, F. E. (2019). *Money and schools* (7th ed.). New York: Routledge.

*Zelman v. Simmons-Harris*, 536 U.S. 639 (2002).

Ziebarth, T. (2019). *Measuring up to the model: A ranking of state public charter school laws*. Washington, DC: National Alliance for Public Charter Schools.

*Zobrest v. Catalina Foothills School District*, 509 U.S. 1 (1993).

# Index

# About the Author

**Dr. Clinton Born** is a thirty-year veteran of public schools where he served as a superintendent of schools, principal, assistant principal, guidance counselor, and teacher. Currently, he is a professor in the Franciscan University of Steubenville graduate education program teaching courses to prepare aspiring public and nonpublic principals and superintendents for licensure. Throughout his distinguished career, he

- stewarded a school district from financial ruin to fiscal stability;
- passed a 10.98 mil operating levy with the highest passage rate in district history;
- applied for and secured numerous grants, including federal entitlement applications; and
- designed and delivered a variety of online graduate education courses.